THE DIVINE PLAN
B E Y O N D
2012

Caroline Cory

OMnium Books

The Divine Plan: Beyond 2012

Caroline Cory

Copyright © 2007 by Caroline Cory

Published by OMnium Books
Palm Beach, FL

All rights reserved. This book may not be reproduced in whole or in part without written permission from the author.

Printed in the United States of America by:
Signature Book Printing,
www.sbpbooks.com

ISBN 978-0-9766116-3-9

For questions or comments about this book, please e-mail info@omniumfoundation.com.

www.omniumfoundation.com

This book is dedicated to...

The Universal Father
My Divine Father

Table of Contents

PREFACE vii

Part I: Introduction

1. The Inevitable Truth, Inevitable Change and Inevitable Divine Intervention 1
2. Creation Principles: Mind Energy, Spirit Energy, Physical Energy 11
3. Time, Dimensional Space and Parallel Existence 35
4. Organization of the Local Universe: the Invisible Government 57

Part II: Unfolding the Divine Plan

5. The Intelligent Beings Involved in the Divine Plan 73
6. The Second Coming 101
7. Birthing a New Species 107
8. Timing of the Divine Plan 117
9. The Geophysical Changes 123
10. Ramifications of the Divine Plan for the Individual .. 133
11. The Unification of Spiritual Trends 141
12. Government and Consciousness 147
13. The Birthing of a New Government 151

Part III: Preparing for the Inevitable: Practical Tools

14. Basic Guidelines for the Upcoming Changes 167
15. Reorganizing Your Thought Process and Belief Systems 171
16. Managing Your Spiritual Beliefs 177
17. Managing Your Physical Body 183
18. Managing Your Career 191
19. Managing Your Home Life 195
20. Managing Your Family and Friends 197

FINAL NOTE 201
GLOSSARY 203
ACKNOWLEDGEMENTS 207

Preface

Who are we and what are we doing here? What is humanity's destiny and what will happen in 2012 or perhaps 100 years from now? What is our individual task in humanity's evolution? When we ask these questions, we begin to implement the cause and effect suggested in the very questioning. If we are asking, it implies that we do not know the answer. If we do not know the answer to these questions about our future, it is because the answer does not exist or is yet to be created. If something has already been created or manifested, then we will all acknowledge its existence and will thus have no reason for inquiring about it. So, in that sense, we are embarking on a journey that is now being created, and by asking the questions regarding our possible or probable future, we are also implementing its manifestation!

2012 is also a reality that is being created. It is the *continuation* of our current reality into its next evolutionary stage – an event no different than those in previous historical times when man predicted "the end of the world" or "the end of life as we know it." 2012 is *not* a return to the enlightened eras of ancient civilizations but rather the creation of a *new and unprecedented era* that is yet to be birthed on the Earth. Through these pages, you will realize that the emergence of this New Era is not only imminent but also inevitable and necessary. Also, this age is significantly unique in that it entails the full consciousness awakening of a group of beings for the purpose of actively instigating and participating in this new reality on Earth. These beings, who are orchestrating and leading the tremendous changes upon the Earth, have simultaneously arrived to uplift the planet into a new dimensional field. While this plan involves the *entire humanity*, it is the collective landing of these beings that is of particular importance and is what makes 2012 a unique and unprecedented event in the history of the material worlds.

I will discuss these details and more in the following chapters, but, first, I would like to mention that the information contained in this book is the result of *direct experiences* with other worlds and realities that exist beyond our Earth and Milky Way perimeters. This material is not based on rational conclusions drawn from various teachings, ancient scripts or other metaphysical books. The experiences I speak of are the result of a spontaneous *merging of all my human senses* – hearing, seeing, sensing – with the very material detailed in this book in such a way as to leave me no doubt about its truth or validity. These powerful experiences, which I call *total knowing* or *know-sis*, spontaneously occur when my human mind transfers into an alternate communication channel or circuit – that of the divine mind.

I say "spontaneous" as this process does not require being in a deep trance-like meditative state. Rather, a self-learned process of *mind discernment* allows me to tap into the highest frequencies available within this universe and beyond in a clear and precise manner. Such work – the deliberate transfer between mind circuits – is not the work of a medium or a channel, of which I am neither, but that of any human who is willing to acknowledge such inherent divine ability and stretch his/her mind *in the proper way* to these extended areas of awareness. Therefore, I wish to emphasize that the material that follows is not from a source or entity outside my being. The ones who speak here are particles or extensions of my current physical being *or the parts of my consciousness that are still merged with Source* and that exist simultaneously in the far distant universal core – or more specifically, in the area of the Central Universe[1] over 100 billion light years away. These various particles of my being participate simultaneously or intermittently in the transcription and translation of this information. For this reason, I will address the reader in the second person as it is transcribed from Source. Any human is capable of such a task – of connecting with Source information – provided s/he knows of this capability and is taught accordingly. In fact, our human birth right presupposes expanding our consciousness with such precision and control for the purpose of connecting deliberately and directly to our Spirit Self[2] and to our original Source.

---

1 See figure 1 on page xi.
2 The aspect of our self permanently connected with Source.

My experience with other realities, contact with Source and this form of total knowing commenced at a young age when I began communicating telepathically with various spirit beings who appeared to be of similar lineage as my own. I was able to identify this lineage by the clear impression that we were one and the same, or that I was an extension of them in physical form. Little did I know at the time, however, that through this process of communication my consciousness was expanding into unfathomable realms of reality and my mind channels were being reorganized in such a way as to become able to reach far away distances within the universe. In my book *GOD Among Us: Inside the Mind of the Divine Masters*, I explain in detail the gradual progression of this process of mind expansion that contributed greatly to my earthly awakening. I share many instances, such as predictions, spontaneous healings and instant materialization, which supported the validity of this communication process. Similarly, many have experienced directly in my classes and workshops the concepts discussed in my books – such as the different forms of energy and their arrangement within the universe or the various types of beings – which further verifies the validity of the information I receive from Source. So, for the purpose of clarity, I am proceeding here with a similar approach – that of direct connection to Source reality – and transcribing these experiences with as much accuracy as possible through the use of a human language. It remains the choice of the reader, however, to judge the validity and relevance of the information provided and the guidance being offered in this book.

While my purpose in writing this book is to include as much helpful information as possible, I chose to omit certain details that may jeopardize the application and proper manifestation of those events that have global impact. I will, however, share this information in separate newsletters or possibly through a future publication. Also, due to the complexity, massiveness and multi-dimensionality of this information, it is a difficult task to transcribe this sort of material in a simplistic and linear fashion. Therefore, it is recommended that you simply allow your mind to open to the Source that speaks to you here and let the information register and unfold within your consciousness on its own terms and at its own pace.

The purpose of this book is to enlighten the reader about the impending New Era in the history of humanity. The book serves to address the different aspects of this era that are manifesting multi-dimensionally – not just those visible material changes – and shed light on how to best prepare for such tremendous change. To this end, I chose to divide the book into 3 parts in order to allow the information transcribed herein to become integrated in your consciousness in a multi-dimensional manner. As such, Part I explains the relationship between Source and Earth and the process by which they are perpetually connected. While this section may appear somewhat technical, it serves to create the framework for the information in the later parts of the book and to depict the multi-dimensionality of Creation – at Source as well as in our own material world – while portraying our inevitable interconnectivity. On a subliminal level, the reading of this first part allows the opening of your consciousness to occur naturally as you align your focus with that of Source. Part II describes the actual changes of the New Era on various levels and as they occur, namely the appearance of divine beings on the Earth, the geophysical, astronomical and electromagnetic changes and the governmental upsets, among other possible disruptions and transformations. The later segment of Part II describes the way our future will appear, which includes the birthing of a new species and a new reality altogether on the earth plane. Finally, Part III offers practical tools regarding how to best prepare for this great transition time that is ahead of us with grace, intelligence and responsibility.

Also, as you read these pages, know that the questions that you may have at first will most likely be answered in a later portion of the book and that it may require several readings to fully grasp the multi-layered and complete picture drawn in this text. Through this process, however, you will be spontaneously activating your own remembrance and connection to Source as well as the recollection of your unique role within the grand Divine Plan unfolding on the Earth now. Regardless of your individual process, my wish is that you embrace these words and experience the great love and blessings that are encoded herein.

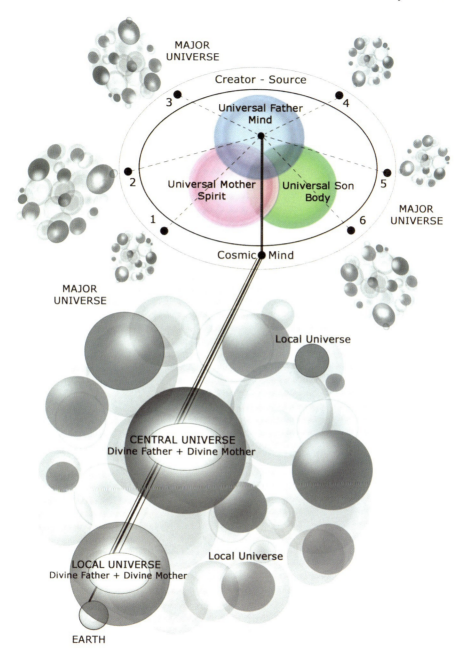

Figure 1: Location of the Local Universe, the Central Universe, and the Creator-Source in relation to the Earth.

Part I

Introduction

1

The Inevitable Divine Intervention

In the beginning, this universe was a nebula that through the process of divine creation accumulated enough speed and momentum to attract the appropriate materials and energies that engender life as you now know it. Earth, with all your oceans and seas combined, has the approximate size of a needle head, comparatively speaking, and is one minute aspect of the nebula's countless manifestations. Earth is part of the original nebula and, by this very fact, complies with an original creative blueprint that is of a divine nature. The divine blueprint[3] dictates a permanent state of Love, Truth, Beauty and Goodness, or what may resemble pure positive energy on your world. If this blueprint becomes disrupted by unknown[4] circumstances, the tainted portions eventually dislodge themselves from the whole and the rest of the created nebula. It is at this point of dislodging and at this fraction of time that we are speaking. This time constitutes the

---

3 As originally created by the Divine Creator of the Local Universe.
4 Not in harmony with the divine vibration.

events of 2012 and beyond – a time that has accumulated enough momentum that it can neither be ignored nor avoided.

Let us assume, for a moment, that no one on this earth plane is willing to accept such truth. Well then, it would be admissible to conclude that no one will actually experience any of the events we discuss in this book, since all beings, through their own birth right,[5] create their own destiny and reality according to their belief systems. If you do not believe in or even know of these events, then this time – 2012 and beyond – is not an option for you to consider and therefore create. However, at this moment in Earth's history the Divine Plan must be restored. It is at this juncture of restoration that we intended this book to be written so as to explain why humanity is now being "intervened with" to a certain degree, regardless of your individual belief system or that on which you are focused. It seems to be a contradiction in terms to say "Divine Plan" and "intervened with" in the same sentence, as the Divine Plan is based on free, un-intervened or un-interfered with, will. However, this restoration of the Divine Plan is a necessary response to the Earth's and humanity's request to re-establish their original divine blueprint. Through this plan, the disruptive trends that have ruled this world and kept humanity a captive of fear, misguided and oblivious to its divine blueprint for millennia at a time, will be annihilated. In this sense alone, the Divine Plan is leading the destiny of this Earth so that even those who do not believe in such an event will nonetheless experience a tremendous reality shift that is orchestrated by the Divine Order – the Creator Order that creates all intelligent life on this earth plane and beyond. Simply put, this is a time of *divine intervention* that will allow the manifestation of the New Era of Love and Light. This era manifests through the multi-dimensional implanting of new energy patterns, unprecedented geophysical changes as well as the emergence of the Divine Father and His flawless mission within your time and space reality.

---

5   The free will and right of every created being to create his/her own destiny through focused thought.

THE REASON ...

Over 200,000 years ago, the reigning planetary beings supervising your Earth created the reality in which many humans are still living today. Through their own free will, these beings consciously and deliberately chose to limit you, manipulating your consciousness and keeping you captives of a fear-based, control-based system. These beings instilled a plan based on illusion and separateness, cloaking the Earth within its own deceptive veils. Such accounts have appeared sporadically in various texts throughout your history and while they are based on truth, the interpretation of such truth is somewhat clouded by human misunderstanding and judgment.

The planetary beings that supervise and assist your Earth's evolution are Divine Sons of the 3rd order as these beings are the most apt at integrating physically within the material realms. However, such close proximity to a juvenile material species can occasionally entice a Planetary Supervisor to err. Such tragic occurrence begins with simple curiosity and experimentation but may eventually lead to dangerous abuses of free-will as well as conceited and narcissistic acts. In the entire history of the many billions-of-years-old Creation, such rebellious or tragic events have only occurred 3 times upon a new world such as your Earth. With each incidence, the rebellion isolates that world from Source for a time but is subsequently reversed through the intervention and manifestation of the Divine Father within the world in question.

The ways in which the Planetary Supervisors are able to isolate a new planet from the rest of Creation are manifold. While Mind and Spirit Energy of Source cannot be manipulated by any created being other than the Divine Father / Mother, these energies can be blocked or interfered with so as to allow only small portions to be received by the inhabited planet. Since Mind and Spirit Energies utilize the transport and communication channels of the grid system, occupying strategic locations within the channels or axes where Mind and Spirit energies enter the earth plane allows such interference to take place. In addition to obstructing these entry points, the re-direction of the very channels and axes also creates confusion and blockages and impedes humans attempting to access the higher realms or the outer worlds. Many such vortexes and axes on the Earth have either been re-directed improperly or destroyed entirely. These malevolent manipulations of the earth grid system are the reason for which humans have been unable to receive proper guidance from Source directly and with clarity or precision.

Physical Energy, on the other hand, can be manipulated within a material world more drastically, allowing an entire experience and reality to exist outside the divine flow for a time. Such process happens through the re-configuration of the very physical aspects of the earth grid, which automatically affects the experience of life on Earth. The original earth grid structure was conceived and built according to divine geometry, which is infinite. However, it can be physically amended so as to become a finite structure. As such, your original earth grid, which was a hexagonal formation of infinite potential, was broken and reduced by your previous Planetary Supervisors to the limited and finite dodecahedron reality in which you currently exist. The implications of such alteration in shape and structure are tremendous as the original shapes and structures contain the very vibration and intelligent design of the Divine Creator. What appears to be a minor omission within a geometric shape corresponds, in fact, to a massive "error" in terms of frequency and vibrational reality. The human brain functioning, for example, which is correlated with the proper organization and structure of the grid system, suddenly becomes restricted and disturbed. The current reality of separateness, selfishness and greed are but a few byproducts of such limited understanding of truth and multi-dimensional existence.

Since the appearance of the finite dodecahedron on your Earth over 200,000 years ago, your previous Planetary Supervisors also instilled spiritual concepts and teachings that summon the worship and fear of an unattainable "God." They taught you to believe, through the use of mind control, that you are unable to reach your Divine Creator directly, unable to be free of human limitations, unable to experience the spirit energy of Love, Truth, Beauty and Goodness or to remember your divine heritage without struggle and pain. Needless to say, such teachings are not only erroneous but also constitute a treacherous breach of the universal laws instilled by your Divine Creator. The manipulative beings who instilled your false reality have now been incapacitated and no longer have authority, so to speak, to function within this realm. However, those who believe in their existence continue to carry similar destructive beliefs. They are still misleading others and holding the Earth's energetic plane at a very low vibration. This long-drawn negative energy accumulated enough momentum that the intervention of your Divine Parent was finally required to restore and reclaim the harmony and balance of your planet.

THE INEVITABLE CHANGE ...

By definition, energy has momentum and a *potential outcome*. Your thoughts, which are Mind Energy, exist in a *potential* spectrum of reality – the world of probability[6] – and eventually materialize in this 3-dimensional layer of reality. Similarly, collective destructive energy has accumulated and created momentum over thousands of years on the earth plane. It has also created a potential outcome that must materialize at one point in time and space. The projection of such materialization can be likened to a birthing process where the due date is somewhat accurate yet *inevitable* and simply bound to materialize. The potential and probable outcome of this accumulated destructive energy is now on the verge of materializing in the next years to come. The years between 2008 and 2012 are the projected and approximate timing for the actualization of this potential. This actualization is unavoidable and non-negotiable. *However, the conditions or ways in which such actualization will affect humanity is dependent upon your individual belief systems and your individual decision making ability. Therefore, the repercussions of these conditions are still being created by your own free will.*

Concurrently, as destructive energy accumulates through the ages, so does divine energy. Since all worlds are created from the same divine fabric and remain interconnected, it follows that all are based on the same principles and share common divine heritage and attributes, regardless of what is observed on the physical plane. When a world becomes isolated due to accumulated destructive

---

[6] Frequency range where thoughts are accumulated in order to reach enough momentum to allow material manifestation. For more details, refer to the book "The Visible and Invisible Worlds of GOD."

patterns, it reaches a *limit* where these destructive patterns can no longer coexist with the divine patterns or blueprint with which this world was originally created. *2012 is the time when these 2 energy trends – destructive and divine – can no longer co-exist.* A new world must indeed be created and birthed at this moment in time.

IS DIVINE INTERVENTION INTERFERING WITH HUMAN FREE WILL? ...

Physical beings of human and non-human origin infiltrate the earth plane while also remaining invisible[7] for the purpose of influencing the outcome of the collective mind matrix. However, no being is powerful enough to do such a thing – influence another's mind – unless allowed to do so by the individual in human form. Additionally, invisible beings with "negative" influence are no different than your visible friends or acquaintances who exert manipulative powers over you. Realizing this, it is important that your thoughts be your own and that you act consciously and deliberately according to your own free will.

Spirit beings aligned with Source, on the other hand, allow human expression and thought to expand according to the human free will. Therefore, they usher humanity towards its highest good. These spirit beings act as *spiritual parents*, so to speak, of the human species. It is at this point of ushering and parenting that we must clarify the extent to which spirit beings from Source are *contributing* to human expansion and the extent to which they may appear as *interfering* with its free will.

While spirit beings of Source regard human free will as an innate birth right, they are also shaping new understanding and assisting humanity in manifesting a new consciousness on the earth plane. In order to avoid the confusion caused by the semantics of the human language, let us consider for a moment the difference between "assisting" and "interfering" as it is understood through human perception. If a child who is clearly in imminent physical danger is allowed by his/her parent to express his/her free will by jumping off a cliff, for

---

7   These physical beings exist within the earth plane but remain in another layer of reality or "dimension" and therefore remain invisible.

example, that parent may be regarded as irresponsible, immoral and possibly insane. If, however, the parent interferes with the child's free will and saves the child's life, the parent may be regarded as a noble hero. Which perception is truly accurate? How do you determine the morality of such an act? In which case are you *allowing* the free will of your child and in which case are you *interfering*?[8]

Similarly, it is a matter of perception to consider that your spirit parent may, in fact, be interfering with your free will in order to instigate wholesome decision making on your part. At what point is the spirit parent regarded as a noble hero? There is no right or wrong answer to this line of questioning as each individual is allowed to express his/her will according to his/her own individual perception and belief system. In fact, there are as many perceptions and belief systems as there are individual beings on this Earth. There is, however, *a limit* at which all belief systems and perceptions come to an agreement. This limit is reached when the *conscious and deliberate intent* of an individual allows him/her to harm another. This fact, in all cases and from all perspectives, calls for the interference or intervention of a parent or authority figure. Had this child been subjected to deliberate harm by another, then the parent's interference will universally and unquestionably be applauded.

It is at this point of Earth's history that we are now speaking, as a portion of humanity has *consciously and deliberately caused harm* to many others for millennia at a time. It is at this juncture in your evolution that your spirit parent is assisting, affecting or interfering with – whatever you choose to call it or perceive it as – your free will in order to halt the harm that has been consciously done to you. In this case, your spirit parent can only be regarded as a noble hero, indeed.

You must also realize that your spirit parent carries the energy of the Divine Creator, that which is based on Love, Truth, Beauty and Goodness. In that respect, your spirit parent can only be of the highest good. Therefore, by acknowledging the inherent nature of your divine parent, your human confusion and quandary regarding the appropriateness of this divine intervention simply dissolve and the line of endless questioning automatically becomes irrelevant.

---

8   A "child" may be substituted with a "friend addicted to drugs" to illustrate further the point made above.

YOUR ROLE IN THE DIVINE PLAN …

It is essential to realize that divine intervention implies a plan that is orchestrated by highly evolved beings of various divine orders who execute such plan with flawless precision – regardless of the immediate physical outcome you may perceive. More importantly, it is crucial to understand that this plan involves *each one of you*. This means that you, as an individual being in human form, are instrumental to this plan being carried out. Your individual awakening and mind expansion, regardless of your age, sex, race or physical location, allows the divine flow to exist in human form and become anchored within the earth plane. Therefore, the accounts discussed in this book do not imply that you should sit back and allow others to lead the show, so to speak, but, rather, you must engage fully – more so than ever before! – in the execution of this plan on the earth plane. Remember, your physical being *is* the vessel for this divine flow. By simply allowing yourself to embrace your own divinity and allowing this flow to exist, *you* will be working intimately with the Divine Father and the highest Divine Order in Creation and contributing greatly to the manifestation of the New Era on the Earth.

Note

While for simplicity I refer to the Divine Father as "He," the Divine Son as "He," and the Divine Mother as "She," these divine energies have no true correlation to your human understanding of gender. Human beings may reflect, carry or embody an individual formula of these divine energies regardless of gender. For example, though I refer to the Divine Son as "He," a Divine Son may take the human form of a male or female. The same is true for the Divine Father when He becomes embodied in human or other material form.

2

Creation Principles

All aspects of life derive from one Creator-Source,[9] which is Mind Energy, Physical Energy, Spirit Energy and the combinations of these 3 energies thereof. **Refer to figure 2 on page 12.** Within the realm of Creation, there exist laws and principles that govern each and every one of these energy forms. The details of such laws and principles are not relevant to the scope of this book. Here, however, it is necessary to consider the Creation principles from these 3 inherent aspects – mind-al, spiritual and physical energy – in order to comprehend the nature and purpose of your current existence. We shall attempt to describe, in simplistic terms, the principles of human creation as they apply to the current shift in your Earth's history.

---

[9] Original Creator of All That Is – all of existence.

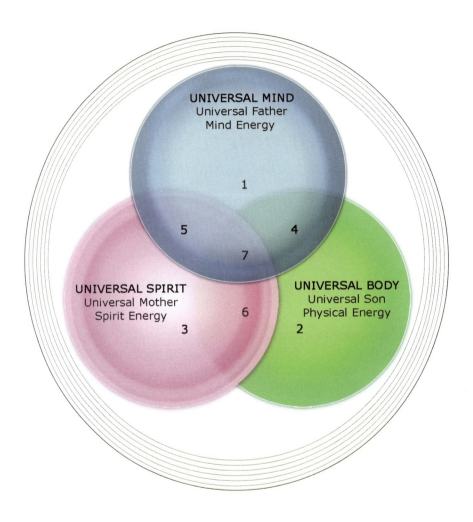

Figure 2: The Creator-Source

The Creator-Source's inherent energy forms – Mind, Spirit and Physical[10] – manifest in infinite possibilities throughout Creation. These countless manifestations derive from one of the 7 possible combinations of the Creator-Source, which are: Mind, Body, Spirit, Mind-Body, Mind-Spirit, Body-Spirit and Mind-Body-Spirit. Each of these energy manifestations varies according to the rate of its vibrational frequency (which defines the speed of energy), its composing atomic elements (which defines the mass of energy) and the rotation cycle about its nucleus (which defines the character or nature of energy). Even though all life must encompass at once Mind, Spirit and Physical Energy to a certain degree, it is the individual combination of these 3 energies and their subsequent arrangement that makes each creation unique. For example, the Divine Father[11] of your Local Universe is the embodiment of the Mind-Body energy of the Creator-Source and carries a unique energetic frequency, mass and movement. The Divine Mother,[12] on the other hand, is the embodiment of Spirit Energy alone and carries Her own unique energetic frequency, mass and movement. Together, they constitute yet another form of energy – the Mind-Body-Spirit energy – and become the Divine Parent of the entire Local Universe that now carries their newly-created formula or, in other words, a new frequency, mass and movement.

THE CREATOR-SOURCE AND THE CREATION OF INTELLIGENT BEINGS ...

While there is no such thing as "hierarchy" in terms of better or worse, which is a human concept, there are nonetheless such things as different types of created beings or species that can perform different duties according to the mass of their consciousness, their nature and their programmed functioning. Those who are larger or have evolved further on their journey typically assist others in the same process.

The attributes inherent within the Creator-Source's own being are pure Love, Truth, Beauty and Goodness and may be likened to pure

---

10   Also referred to as "Body."
11   Original Creator of the Local Universe and all intelligent beings and species therein.
12   Original co-Creator of life within the Local Universe, which includes all intelligent beings and species.

positive energy. These attributes are absolute and perfect, indeed. However, each time Creator-Source creates, a particle of His energy *splits off*, and that particle becomes its own being or consciousness. This newly created consciousness carries a portion of the memory of its Creator and remains eternally connected to Him through an *energetic umbilical cord*.

Species upon species are thus created, and with each creation the particles of the Universal Mind, Body or Spirit split off into more finite[13] consciousness. The more finite a creation, the "smaller" it becomes and the lesser amount of energy it is able to carry due to its remoteness from the original Creator-Source. Also, each intelligent being originates out of a unique formula that characterizes its nature, attributes and functioning. The Universal Mind, for example, is the energy of the original Creator – the inventor, director and visionary of all life. The Universal Mind is also *personalized energy* and can be called the Universal "Father," which refers to a sort of spirit parent rather than simply a mind. The Universal Body is the extension of the Universal Mind / Father and carries the energy of all intelligent beings in existence. Along with the Universal Mind / Father, the Universal Body is the co-Creator of intelligent beings, the physical worlds and also, the manager, administrator and sovereign of the Universal Mind / Father's creations. Since the Universal Body is personalized in the second being of Creation, He can be referred to as the *Universal Son*. The Universal Spirit is yet another extension of the Universal Mind / Father. She, on the other hand, carries the energy of life itself as it is experienced through the physical worlds and intelligent beings. The Universal Spirit is personalized in the third being of Creation and can also be referred to as the *Universal Mother*.

As universes upon universes are created, the personality, energy and characteristics of the Universal Mind, Body and Spirit – and their combinations thereof – are distributed throughout Creation according to a divine intelligent design and plan. At the conception of a Major Universe,[14] the Divine Father and Divine Mother appear at the Central Universe of that massive cluster as a replica of the original Creator-Source yet carrying their own characteristics. This Divine Father of the Major Universe is the embodiment of the Universal Father

---

13 "Finite" is used here to describe a smaller portion or aspect of consciousness rather than "fixed" or complete since all created things are infinite.
14 Major universal structure that contains over 100,000 Local Universes. **See figure 1 on page xi.**

and the Universal Son of the Creator Source. He is then the Creator, inventor and visionary *as well as* the administrator, organizer, manager and supreme sovereign of all His created beings and physical worlds. The Divine Mother, on the other hand, is the embodiment of the Universal Spirit and thereby carries the energy that supports all life within the Major Universe. She is the co-Creator and support system of all created beings and physical worlds.

Similarly, within your Local Universe there exist one Divine Father and Divine Mother who are the original Creators of your worlds. While they are a close replica of the Divine Father / Mother of the Central Universe, they nonetheless become a magnificent new form of energy that is distributed throughout your entire universe. **Refer to figure 1 on page xi.**

MIND ENERGY…

Mind Energy begins at the Source and represents the first aspect of the Creator-Source. This energy is distributed throughout Creation through the magnificently complex system of the *Cosmic Mind* that revolves around this first center of Creation. The Cosmic Mind requires 3 separate channels to travel through space and is, in fact, personalized, embodied, directed and managed by divine beings who connect Mind Energy from the first center to the center of each Major Universe. The divine beings who embody Mind Energy become the direct link between the Creator-Source and its respective Major Universe where Mind Energy is then distributed through all of the universes encircling the Central Universe. Finally, this same Mind Energy now embodied by the Divine Creator of the Major Universe is carried forth to the local universes through the embodiment of yet another divine being – the Divine Father of the Local Universe. From Earth, you are able to experience Mind Energy by aligning and connecting your physical energy with the being of the Divine Father of your Local Universe. **See figure 3 on page 16.**

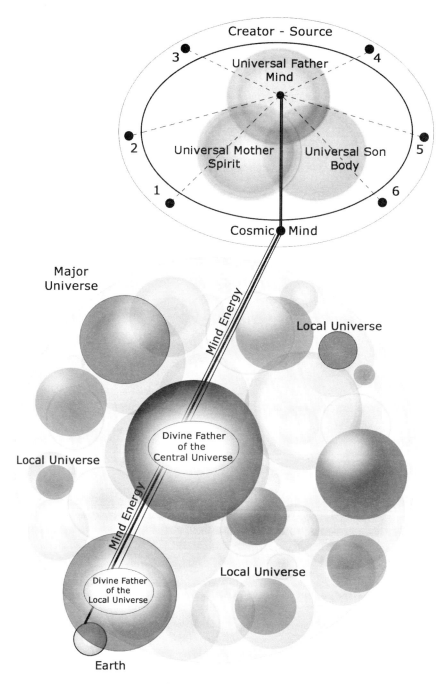

Figure 3: Distribution of Mind Energy from the Creator- Source to the Local Universe and Earth.

Your Divine Father is an infinitely complex multi-dimensional Being who creates through His thought or through Mind Energy. Subsequently, this becomes the *process of creation* for all intelligent beings within His universe.

Mind Energy within your Local Universe is also the energy that sustains all of the minds in existence, from the mind of the physical worlds to the minds of the created intelligent beings inhabiting them. "Sustain" in this context means to keep all minds interconnected according to specific principles and attributes as well as through actual physical *circuits* that continuously transfer information from one mind to another. And due to the astounding expanse of the universes, Mind Energy travels billions of light years between systems faster than the speed of light in order to link up the entire stream of Creation – from the original Creator-Source to the center of your Local Universe and, in turn, your planetary system and each individual being therein. Therefore, a mind-al navigation system or communication circuitry is established for each planet, each star, each galaxy and each universe that link up to adjacent universes and so on and so forth, until all become part of one uniform Mind Energy matrix connected at the Central Universe and, in turn, at the Creator-Source.

THE FUNCTIONS OF MIND ENERGY ...

Mind Energy is the generator of consciousness. It contains all thoughts in existence and is capable of generating all the possible and probable formulas for Creation. Mind Energy functions on the basis of a trigonometric arrangement or formula, which means it manifests in 3-fold applications throughout Creation. In your physical reality, the trigonometric attributes allow the convergence of other forms of energy, namely spiritual and physical, for the purpose of perpetually interacting in a cohesive and steadfast manner. When Mind Energy is displayed as the main circuit being utilized or stimulated, the Spirit and Physical Energies comply with such demand and become "co-tangents," so to speak. Conversely, when Spirit Energy is being utilized, then Mind and Physical Energy become the co-tangents of this new formula. The trigonometric aspect of Mind Energy is malleable and adaptable through a zero transfer point that exists at the junction of each channel and all subsequent sub-channels. This spontaneous zero point[15] transfer process allows you to integrate the properties of all forms of energies and discern the interaction of the energies that are being utilized at any given time.

In a human context, the physical brain contains within its essence the same trigonometric property, allowing the perfect interaction and balance of various cosmic connections through 3 separate channels: planetary, inter-galactic and trans-universal. This means that when you are on Earth, you are part of the collective human mind matrix that is proportionally trigonometric to the Milky Way mind matrix, which is then part of your universe mind matrix, which is then part of a multi-universal mind matrix – all of which are connected through the same proportionate trigonometric functions. When focused on the human collective mind matrix, the galactic and universal channels become the co-tangents, so to speak, or *functions of* the main channel being utilized. Conversely, when focused on the galactic Mind Energy channel, the planetary and universal channels become the co-tangents or functions of the channel being utilized. The reason for such a discernment process is so that one can remain focused on one reality at a time for the purpose of accomplishing a task. Since the human mind is still somewhat under-developed, this trigonometric attribute of the human brain functioning allows the relinquishing of other forms of consciousness for a time – until the conscious re-alignment or opening of all 3 channels to Source can be achieved in a gradual and controlled manner. Once the opening of all 3 Mind Energy channels occurs in human form, you are able to discern and transfer your thoughts from the planetary to the galactic channel or the universal channel for the purpose of retrieving specific information with accuracy and precision. **See figures 4 and 5 on pages 19 and 20.**

---

15   Areas within physical space and throughout Creation that allow the collapse, recreation, transmutation and regeneration of energy.

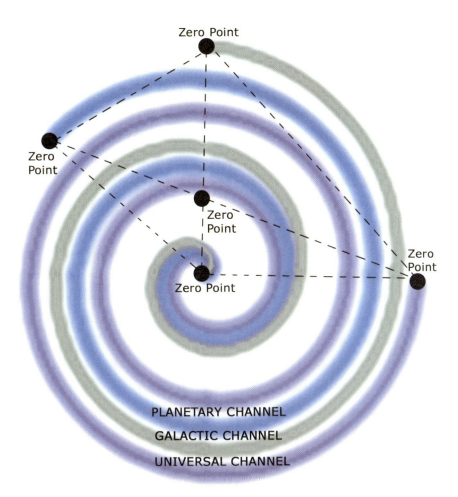

Figure 4: Trigonometric functions of Mind Energy.

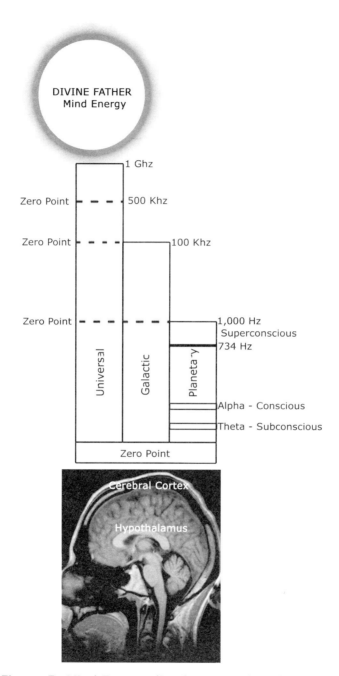

Figure 5: Mind Energy distribution within the human brain.

MIND ENERGY IN THE HUMAN BODY ...

Mind Energy is the first aspect of Source and holds the divine blueprint within it. When a Divine Being embodies the energy of the Universal Mind / Father, He becomes the embodiment of its blueprint or DNA. As He travels from the Central Universe into the Local Universe, He brings forth the atomic elements of this original formula throughout the universal journey. And as this blueprint unfolds through space, the trigonometric aspects of this original formula unfold in a spectacular system of circuitry resembling the double helix format of the human DNA. **See figure 6 on page 22.**

Once implanted in your Local Universe, Mind Energy is distributed from the Divine Father into your system through a similar double-helix light beam circuit. This circuit encircles the entire universe and pours into your planetary system and Earth through many doorways or channels that transcend the time / space continuum. The main doorways within your Local Universe correlate with the 12 faces of the *current* dodecahedron[16] of your earth grid and subsequently the human energy field. Once in your energy field, Mind Energy enters the human body through the cerebral cortex, then the limbic system, then the hypothalamus, which distributes it evenly throughout the body by way of the endocrine and the nervous systems. Mind Energy's connection within the human body is the pineal gland, which is responsible for light absorption and light refraction. Mind Energy corresponds to the mind-personality-creativity of the Divine Father and is part of your unique divine DNA formula. Mind Energy is what you call *consciousness*. **See figure 7 on page 23.**

---

16   A geometric shape that has 12 regular **pentagonal** faces, 20 vertices and 30 edges.

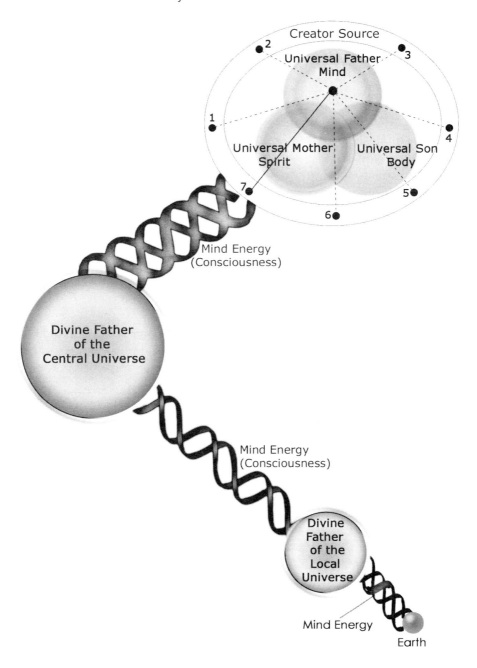

Figure 6: Distribution of Mind Energy from the Creator-Source and throughout the universe.

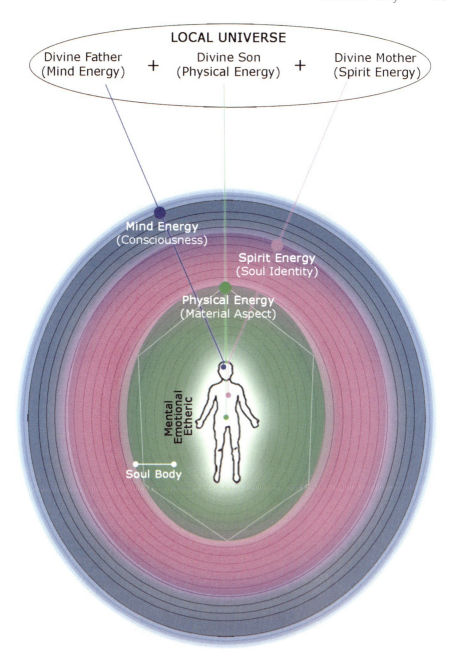

Figure 7: Distribution of Mind, Spirit and Physical Energy embodied in human form.

While Mind Energy can be detected and measured within physical reality, it is not a physical energy. Its true nature, character and attributes cannot be understood by the human mind or through physical instruments. The only possible way to *truly* comprehend such energy is from within its point of origin – the core of your Local Universe. From your current perspective, however, you may experience such energy through the process of mind expansion and alignment or blending with the energy of the Divine Father.[17]

The *effects or repercussions* of Mind Energy within your physical reality, on the other hand, can be measured somewhat accurately, so long as they are recognized as the *perceived aspects* of this Mind Energy and not the actual properties of Mind Energy itself. As such, the mathematical *equivalent* of Mind Energy in a physical system is trigonometric; the geometrical *equivalent* of Mind Energy is tetrahedral; the electromagnetic *equivalent* of Mind Energy ranges from 100KHz to infinity; the vibrational appearance of Mind Energy is *equivalent* to a mixture of silver, blue and white; and Mind Energy's main connection within the human body is through the pineal gland, while its connection with Spirit and Physical Energy in the human body is in the heart center.

SPIRIT ENERGY ...

Spirit Energy begins at the Source and represents the third aspect of the Creator-Source. Spirit Energy is distributed throughout Creation through the magnificently complex system of the *Cosmic Spirit* that revolves around this first center. The Cosmic Spirit is then personalized, embodied, directed and managed by 7 beings who connect Spirit Energy from the First Center to the center of each Major Universe. Each Cosmic Spirit Being becomes the direct link between the Creator-Source and its respective Major Universe where Spirit Energy is then distributed through all of the universes encircling the Central Universe. Finally, this same Spirit Energy – now embodied by the Divine Creator at the Central Universe – is carried forth to your local universes through the being of *the Divine Mother*. When in human form, you are able to experience Spirit Energy by aligning and

---

17   This process is explained in Part III of this book.

connecting your physical energy with the being of the Divine Mother of your Local Universe. **See figure 8 on page 26.**

Spirit Energy allows the *nature and attributes* of the Creator-Source to be embedded within all created beings and things. While there exists an unfathomable number of created life forms, each individual one contains its own identity or *soul* in conjunction with the same divine principles and attributes of Source. These attributes can be described as Love, Truth, Beauty and Goodness and are interpreted according to the corresponding system or location in which each creation occurs. For humanity, Love, Truth, Beauty and Goodness are the divine attributes with which you have originally been formulated. While they may or may not be continuously translated, observed or understood within your physical reality, these are nonetheless the ingredients of your divine genetic makeup and original blueprint.

While Mind Energy is the creative and directional aspect of Source, Spirit Energy is its nurturing aspect and manifests throughout creation as *the breath of life*. Without breath, life cannot be sustained. Breath does not only apply to intelligent creatures but also to the entire physical creation including space. All points of space are sustained by and through Spirit Energy, which allows a synchronized movement and coordination of physical, mind-al and spiritual energy to occur infinitely. As such, your space is filled with invisible matter that holds this very programming and permits the entire space to breathe continuously. While you may observe your galaxy expanding infinitely, it is simply "exhaling," so to speak, and, when it reaches its limits of expansion, it begins to deflate or "inhale," giving the impression of contracting or collapsing. Space breathing is continuous and exponential, which means it continues to adjust infinitely as Creation progresses and manifests new life. At present, space breathing is approximately at the rate of 500,000 years, which means space exhales and expands for 500,000 years and then inhales or retracts for 500,000 years. On an individual level, when perfectly coherent with the breathing of the Earth and, subsequently, the galaxy and outer space, your own physical breathing can allow a spontaneous and immediate expansion to cosmic realities and outer space.

Similar to Mind Energy, Spirit Energy is transferred from one system to another through infinite circuits and grids and is experienced

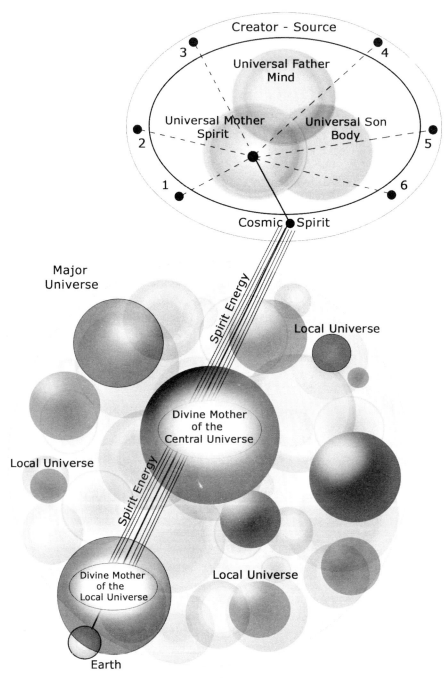

Figure 8: Distribution of Spirit Energy from the Creator-Source to the Local Universe and Earth.

in sequence, so to speak, until a direct link or connection between Earth and Source is established. The mass or size of Spirit Energy that you are able to link up to is dependent upon your consciousness expansion, which is typically gradual and progressive. In other words, the more your consciousness expands, the greater the Spirit Energy you are able to link up to and sustain. Such is also the process of spiritual realization when you, in human form, are finally able to merge or connect with the Spirit Energy of your own Divine Creator at the Source.

Within your Local Universe, Spirit Energy is distributed from the Divine Mother into your system evenly through zero point transfer, transcending the time / space continuum. Spirit Energy not only corresponds to the nature and attributes of the Creator-Source – Love, Truth, Beauty and Goodness – but also to the actual being of the Universal Spirit of Source. This energy is filtered through all the doorways of life and carries the breath, the rhythm and the pulse of the entire Creation into one cohesive and unified energy. Spirit Energy enters your solar system through the Sun and within your individual energy field through your cerebral cortex, then through the limbic system and the hypothalamus, which distributes it evenly throughout the body by way of the endocrine and the nervous systems. Spirit Energy's connection within your body is within the heart center.

While Spirit Energy can be detected and measured within physical reality, it is not a physical energy. The true nature, character and attributes of Spirit Energy cannot be truly grasped or comprehended by the human mind or through physical instruments. The only possible way to *truly* experience and understand such energy is from within its point of origin – the core of your Local Universe. From your human perspective, you may experience Spirit Energy through the process of mind expansion and alignment or blending with the energy of the Divine Mother.[18]

The *effects or repercussions* of Spirit Energy within your physical reality, on the other hand, can be measured somewhat accurately, so long as they are recognized as the *perceived aspects* and not the actual properties of Spirit Energy itself. As such, the mathematical *equivalent* of Spirit Energy in a physical system is a perpetual[19] unit

---

18   See Part III of this book.
19   The perpetual circle is not finite but rather a circle that continuously recreates itself. After the completion of one circle or cycle, each subsequent circle re-generation is never exactly identical to the previously created one.

circle; the geometrical *equivalent* of Spirit Energy is spherical; the electromagnetic *equivalent* of Spirit Energy ranges from 100KHZ to infinity; the *equivalent* vibrational appearance of Spirit Energy is a combination of gold, pink and white colors; and its physical connection to the human body is through the heart and the thymus gland. Spirit Energy is what you call the *soul*. **Refer to figure 7 on page 23.**

PHYSICAL ENERGY ...

Physical Energy is the *expression* or physical manifestation of the Divine Creator's Mind. It manifests as planetary systems, galaxies, universes and all intelligent species within each. From a human perspective, Physical Energy vibrates at slower rates than Spirit or Mind Energy, thereby appearing static or material. However, if observed from the perspective of Source, Physical Energy is perceived as minute particles continuously vibrating. This perpetual vibration is due to the self-regenerating aspect or "fractality" of Physical Energy which allows a continuous regeneration of the atoms that compose the particles of a given physical object. These principles – self-regeneration and fractality – differ from one physical object to the next according to the rotational cycle, speed and shape of the object's composing elements. The diversity in speed, cycle and shape is what allows the design and manifestation of myriad physical creations to become all individually unique. For example, planet Earth is created through Physical Energy with atoms and molecules that allow her to appear round and uphold a certain form of gravity. On the other hand, the human body is composed of the same elements as the Earth's and its atmosphere but is organized in a different arrangement, thereby appearing as it does and performing the duties relevant to its creation. Regardless of their physical appearance or atomic arrangement, the Earth and the human body are nonetheless created through the same Physical Energy that is based on the same principles of self-regeneration and fractality. Therefore, the Earth and the human body sustain a perpetual re-regeneration cycle or you may say that Physical Energy, in its countless manifestation, is a form of energy that is nonetheless *infinite*.

PROPERTIES OF PHYSICAL ENERGY ...

Physical Energy begins at the Source and represents the second aspect of the Creator-Source. This energy is the expression of the Universal Mind and is personalized in what is called the *Universal Son*. Physical Energy is distributed throughout Creation through a magnificently complex system of *Cosmic Gravity* that revolves around this first center. The Cosmic Gravity circuit then appears at the center of the Major Universe and, in turn, at the core of your Local Universe through the being of the Divine Father. From the Divine Father, Physical Energy spreads over an unfathomable grid system that aligns all physical life into one cohesive structure. **See figure 9 on page 30.** It is this Physical Energy of the Universal Son and subsequently your Divine Father that produces and maintains the perpetual gravity, spin, rotation and speed of every molecular physical organism, along with its inherent ability to *self-organize, self-generate, self-maintain, self-calibrate and self-renew.*

In your system, Physical Energy is experienced through the 20 vertices of the *current* dodecahedron of your earth grid and subsequently those within your individual energy field. However, this dodecahedron is now being shifted to a new form and will soon give access to new Physical Energy forms and connections within the human body. Physical Energy enters your energy field through the cerebral cortex, the central nervous system and the skeletal system, and, while it connects with Mind and Spirit Energy in the heart center, its seat is in the navel area. The Physical Energy formula includes all geometrical shapes in existence and dictates the spin, speed, ratio and interrelated proportions of molecular energy within all physical life – namely the correlation between the angles, size and rotation of the human cells with those of the Earth and, subsequently, the solar system.

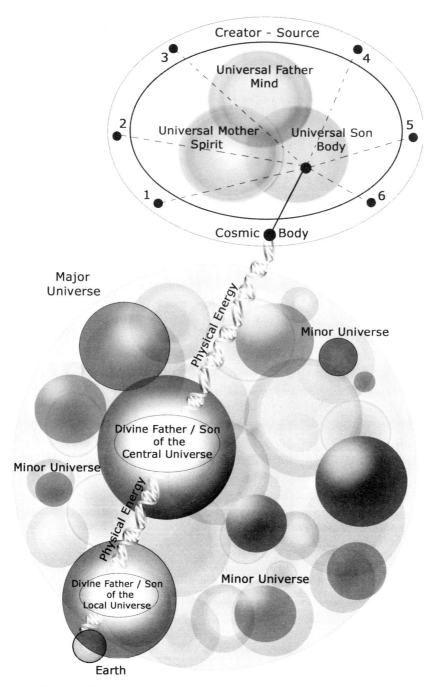

Figure 9: Distribution of Physical Energy from the Creator-Source to the Local Universe and Earth

Physical Energy within your physical reality can indeed be measured accurately to a certain degree, even though your current theories regarding physical life as well as the physical instruments in existence are still limited and somewhat inappropriate. However, it is fair to say that Physical Energy is being explored and expanded at this time. The mathematical *equivalent* of Physical Energy is cubic; the *equivalent* geometrical aspect of Physical Energy contains all geometric shapes in existence; the electromagnetic *equivalent* of Physical Energy ranges from 0.01 Hz to infinity; and the vibrational range relates to yellow and deep green colors. *Physical Energy is a form of energy that is infinite* and is not simply limited to your physical body or the physical worlds you observe; this energy pertains to *physicality* in a wider sense and encompasses the yet to be truly comprehended invisible worlds that are nonetheless physical. These include the worlds of subtle energy, emotions and thoughts to name only a few.

ALL EXISTENCE IS INTERTWINED ENERGY ...

While Mind, Spirit and Physical Energies have separate frequency ranges and channels, they are intertwined in a perfect structure within the cosmos and, subsequently, become assimilated by the human brain and then interconnect through the heart within the physical body. You may say that the heart is the point of transfer between these 3 interconnected channels. In terms of energy polarity, Mind Energy can be described as masculine due to its linear-like, defined and precise force. Spirit Energy is considered feminine, in terms of polarity, due to its circular-like, elliptical and recursive movement. Physical Energy, on the other hand, holds both masculine and feminine forces in order to sustain the wave oscillation of both Mind and Spirit Energy and to manifest them or allow them access into the physical reality.

By definition, all energy – spiritual, mind-al or physical and regardless of its unique manifestation – is *alive*, which means it has a vibration or a movement. What appears to be static energy, such as your material world, for example, is nonetheless energy in motion. The reason the material world appears static is due to the slower speed of its vibration, which gives the *illusion* or impression of it being static. Similarly, thoughts and emotions, which are invisible to you, also constitute a moving energy form that exceeds your human visual spectrum and thus remains imperceptible to you. Thoughts and emotions are nonetheless in existence and are in constant interaction with your physical selves. Therefore, all aspects of energy – visible and invisible – are in constant contact and communication with one another due to their inherent electromagnetic movement. Visible and invisible realities, as a whole, are also continuously interacting, communicating, blending and influencing one another. We say "influencing" because all energy contains information. For example, your seemingly invisible emotions are a form of energy that, when interacting with your physical body, influence your body's chemical or electrical makeup and thereby manifest as a physical symptom of some sort. You become aware of this invisible interaction of energies when your physical body delivers to you a physical sign – or symptom – of such interaction. Similarly, the invisible realms, as a whole, interweave with your physical reality and exchange information continuously whether you recognize this fact instantly or not.

THE INVISIBLE CREATES THE VISIBLE ...

In your physical reality, you create through thought – an energy that you cannot see. You can only see your thought's manifestation when your thought becomes materialized. However, you can be certain that it is your thought that initiated the creation and not vice versa. Your physical brain is unable to create another physical object directly without your thought and the projection of your intent. For example, a red car specific to your liking does not appear outside your door without you having, at some point, initiated the thought of acquiring one. The appearance of the red car means that the invisible energy you utilized – your thought – has now become visible. The visible is then the extension or the material aspect of invisible energy. Or you may say that the invisible energy of thought is the creator force that has manifested physically and not the other way around. The energy creating the visible is therefore the "larger" aspect of the visible. Or, in simple terms, what you can see was created by an energy that you cannot see.

It is a universal understanding that invisible energy creates visible reality. Since the creative process of materialization is innate to all intelligent beings, you may conclude that your physical selves were created by an invisible intelligent energy that is larger than your material self. You are therefore the extension or the material aspect of that larger intelligence. And since all energy is vibrational and interactive, it follows that *you are still permanently connected and interacting with the original thought that has created you*. Through this energetic link to your invisible "parent," you also share its blueprint. Conversely, your invisible parent interacts with, sustains, supports and manages your genetic makeup, your reality and your destiny.

COMMUNICATION BETWEEN THE REALMS ...

The invisible realms co-exist in your physical reality and transfer information to you on multi-dimensional levels through a perpetual umbilical cord. Some information is received as intuition or guidance, some as real perceptions or visions, while some appear in your dream or meditative states. This information is then processed by your human mind and directed outwardly through the projection of your thoughts in order to materialize in one arena or another: artistic, educational, vocational, scientific, etc. Similarly, you – in physical form – are also transferring your material experience back into the invisible realms. Thus, you are continuously co-creating your current reality and adding to the experience of those who have created you. Since the beginning of time, this has been the arrangement and agreement of material creation as Creation is based on the same principle – that all existence is vibrational energy interacting and continuously exchanging information back and forth from one realm to the other.

While the presence of Mind, Spirit and Physical Energy explains the various energy forms in existence, the actual communication process between the worlds occurs through a uniquely designed area called the *Sea of Glass*. This area is summoned for the purpose of producing accurate and transparent universal communication within the entire Creation. The Sea of Glass can be compared to your stadiums, only about 70 times larger, where light or sound trans-universal and inter-galactic communications occur. The main Sea of Glass location is positioned strategically within the Central Universe and is linked to all subsequent satellite Sea of Glass areas within each Local Universe. This massive and extraordinary communication system is not accomplished through a particular language, codes or symbols. It is achieved through *energetic reflectivity*.[20] Reflectivity is the process by which the vibrational field from one area or planet blasts its news and information onto another, which then refracts and reflects onto a surface – the Sea of Glass – in such a way as to be automatically and spontaneously understood by any type of being from any given universe. The energetic reflectivity process is facilitated and maneuvered by the Power Controllers[21] through the use of communication grids that distribute information evenly in and out of the worlds. Once landed on the Sea of Glass surface, all beings, regardless of their origin or location, are able to assimilate the significance of the material being shown. Your Earth's history, for example, has been projected onto this spectacular surface for millennia at a time and countless beings from far-flung universes have followed carefully the main shifts and tremendous events of your planet since its original conception. From an individual perspective, the Sea of Glass and its magnificent reflectivity system are perfectly aligned with the Mind, Spirit and Physical channels that enter your system and subsequently your physical apparatus. This alignment transforms your human existence into an integrated multi-dimensional experience and provides instantaneous outer worldly communication and information transfer. Indeed, it is a most splendid phenomenon that will soon be discovered within your sphere, allowing you, the inhabitants of this Earth, to regain your much anticipated trans-universal citizenship.

---

20   The process by which energetic information is transferred from one point to another.
21   Beings in spirit form responsible for maneuvering energy.

3

Time, Dimensional Space And Parallel Existence

Reality resides within an infinite number of electromagnetic unified fields connected by an infinite number of zero points. What defines reality, however, is the projection of consciousness onto a set of frequency ranges in such a way that everyone sharing such an experience agrees upon the same descriptions, definitions and parameters of this experience. This means that when consciousness, and by extension your physical brain, is directed within a frequency range onto a unified field, your consciousness – or Mind Energy – complies with certain properties previously agreed upon by the creators of this reality. In your awakened hours, your brain is typically focused within a frequency range of 8-30Hz, for example, which allows you to experience an environment that is referred to as "3-dimensional" and that appears material – a fact that everyone in human form has agreed upon. However, when your brain is focused within the frequency range of 2 to 3Hz, for example, all agree to call this other reality "the sleep state." Your consciousness does not collapse or cease to exist as it transitions from one frequency range to another;

it simply applies itself to that vibration and automatically creates a new experience.

Reality, then, is the unique experience that occurs when an individual's brain activity is associated with a specific frequency *range*. We say "range" as it is impossible for you to assign your focus to one single frequency or wavelength since your brain cells are in continuous motion and are unable to pause, so to speak, on a single unit of time or energy. Your experience of reality thus transitions from one state to another or from one experience to another according to the frequency range on which your brain is focused. However, the number of recognizable and acceptable states of reality that you can experience is dictated by *the belief systems* or *agreements* created by the creators of such reality. On Earth, for example, the dream state, deep relaxation state and the alert or higher learning states of reality are the accepted forms of reality, while all other non-measurable[22] states are not. These non-measurable states, which include the experience of other realities while in the awakened state, remain unacceptable or non-complying with the generally agreed upon definition of 3-dimensional reality. On Earth, also, it is generally agreed upon that all machines with 4 wheels are to be called "cars," whereas a round orange juicy food is to be called an "orange." While languages vary from one nation to another, such concepts are bound by a universal agreement and understanding. Such are the current human agreements that have suited humanity for many millennia and supported its need to associate reality with finite and *measurable definitions and common belief systems.* However, reality is not only that which is human-defined. Reality extends to infinite ranges and springs from an infinite number of unified fields merged into one multi-dimensional complex matrix – which is also infinite! In addition, reality is subjective to each individual and is therefore malleable and continuously being created and redefined. No two beings, in human form or otherwise, experience the exact same reality even if tuned to the exact same brain frequency range. Such experience is dependent upon the individual's belief systems, mind and consciousness evolution. There are, therefore, as many realities in existence as there are individual beings accessing, creating or resonating with each reality. When or if humanity at large agrees collectively to reestablish and redefine the parameters and nature of the current 3-dimensional re-

---

[22] Not measurable through electroencephalography or other instruments.

ality, then the 4-dimensional reality and experience will begin to be commonly recognized.

THE EARTH GRID ...

Each created planet holds a grid that serves to distribute Mind, Spirit and Physical Energy throughout its plane according to an original configuration established by the creators of such world. In the case of the Earth, your planetary grid was conceived and established by your Divine Father according to the Physical Energy principles of your Local Universe. As such, your planet's grid consists of 3 intricately intertwined systems: a transport system, a communication system and a time-and-dimensional-space system that distribute Mind, Spirit and Physical Energy of Source throughout the planet in a cohesive manner. The transport system is created to facilitate travel between the earth plane, its neighboring worlds, the Milky Way and the Local Universe. The communication system, on the other hand, allows the transfer of information between the worlds within the galaxy and the universe; whereas the time-and-dimensional-space grid system establishes the layers of reality or "dimensions" within your planet. These 3 grid systems appear as a stupendous matrix of light beams and axes and occupy the space between the surface of the Earth and the outer border of the earth grid, while remaining perpetually joined at the core of the planet. **See figure 10 on page 38.**

Mind Energy uses the transport grid system in order to be present in all areas of the Earth at once. Mind Energy also travels through the communication grid system in order to be received and integrated by all beings on the Earth at once. While, also, Mind Energy travels through the time-and-dimensional-space grid system, allowing it to be incorporated in all layers of reality that exist within the earth plane at once. Similarly, Spirit Energy and Physical Energy utilize the transport system, communication system as well as the time-and-dimensional-space system, becoming fully omnipresent throughout your reality. When all 3 energy forms – Mind, Spirit, Physical – intersect within one grid system, such intersection, or zero point, is called

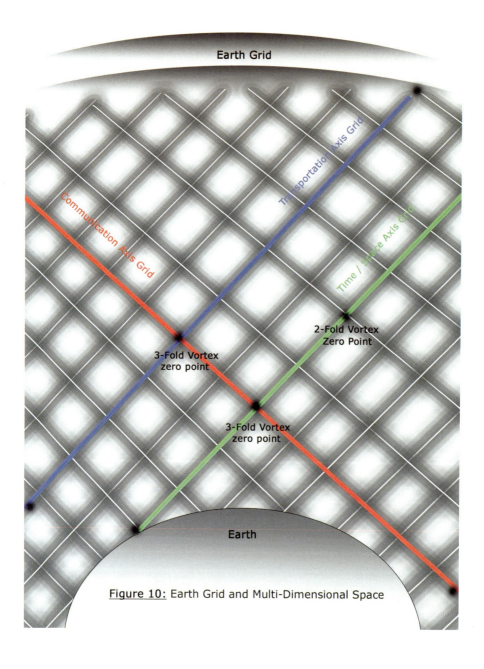
Figure 10: Earth Grid and Multi-Dimensional Space

a 1-fold vortex. When the same 3 energies interconnect with 2 grid systems, such zero intersection point is called a 2-fold vortex. Finally, when Mind, Spirit and Physical Energies are linked with all 3 grid systems, the corresponding zero point is then called a 3-fold vortex. The purpose and careful positioning of the 1, 2 and 3-fold vortexes throughout the Earth allow the integration of universal information in a unique and organized manner. The more energy forms and grid systems are overlapped, the more highly charged the corresponding area on the Earth becomes. As such, the area known as the Bermuda Triangle, the region of the Sea of Japan and those falling between 34° and 35° latitude and 34° and 35° longitude are among the 2-fold and 3-fold vortexes that are highly charged with universal energy. Such tremendous magnetic power allows the more massive divine entities and beings to enter the earth plane and establish new forms of life, instill new information or DNA for a new species, among many other vital tasks.

From an individual perspective, the entire multi-dimensional grid system of the Earth, which includes myriad axes, zero points and manifold vortexes, corresponds perfectly with the organization of the human brain. As such, each aspect of the human brain is actively supported by an equivalent grid line, axis or vortex within the grid system, allowing the individual to experience earthly reality as multi-dimensional. However, in the event a grid line, axis or vortex becomes tampered with or destroyed, its corresponding match in the human brain also becomes inactive – limiting the human experience and alienating it entirely from Mind, Spirit and Physical Energy of Source. Such is the case for your Earth, where beings with negative intent have deliberately corrupted your grid system, limiting your reality to a 3-dimensional experience. It is now the time, however, when the broken grid lines and axes of the Earth become mended, finally reestablishing the direct lines of connection and communication with your divine parents at the Source.

THE MULTI-DIMENSIONAL EXISTENCE ...

Humanity lives in a layer of reality that can be described as 3-dimensional. This reality is observed and experienced through sensory perception and is regarded as "real." On the other hand, what the spirit realm calls *real* is that which is permanently aligned with Source Energy, an energy that is *infinite*. Since your human 3-dimensional experience is ephemeral, it is not "real" but a *virtual experience* that is created when your mind is temporally focused within the specific 3-dimensional layers of reality. Because all life – which includes physical life – is infinite, then your 3-dimensionality is part of another larger reality, maybe 4-dimensional, 5-dimensional or perhaps 32-dimensional and so on and so forth. Clearly, it is the larger reality that includes the smaller ones and not the other way around.

Such perception opens you to many speculations and much new information. If there is multiple-dimensionality, how many dimensions are there within the earth plane? How are these dimensions experienced or demonstrated? Are humans capable of experiencing multiple realities or multi-dimensionality at once? This could become an endless series of questioning until you realize that dimensionality is relative to *consciousness and mind expansion*. The bigger or more evolved a consciousness is, the more it is able to experience simultaneous dimensions or layers of reality. In other words, all created beings – human or otherwise – exist in a spectrum of energy and multiple unified fields, and their ability to experience reality is dependent upon the size or mass of their consciousness. Therefore, expanding one's consciousness is the way by which *all beings* consciously become multi-dimensional.

As a human, you are able to experience your 3-dimensional world as well as the 4th and the 5th dimensions so long as you know of their existence. As you begin your human life, you are taught to focus on your 3-dimensionality alone, that which you perceive through the commonly recognized human senses and belief systems. But as you grow spiritually, your consciousness also expands as to allow a 4th, 5th or 6th dimensional experience. Technically, you need not stop focusing on one in order to open up to the other. Your expansion can be simultaneous but is, in fact, gradual until it reaches 32 layers. In other words, on the earth plane the human experience is *currently* a 32-

dimensional experience and when you become able to experience all 32 layers of reality *at once*, your multi-dimensional experience *in physical form* becomes unnecessary[23] – as you would have then mastered all possible reality layers contained within the human reality spectrum.

Such is the process of the Divine Sons and Masters who have come, time and time again, to teach you this very process of experiencing multi-dimensionality in human form. Once your consciousness allows you to experience a 32-dimensional experience on Earth, you become a Master, a being who has mastered the human condition. It then becomes your choice to remain in human form and continue experiencing all available layers of reality at once or to translate to another non-human reality altogether.

TIME AND DIMENSIONAL SPACE …

Time is a function of physical space, which means time divides space into several pockets or layers of reality or that which you call "dimensions." The *linear* time that is observed on your planet is the result of a human agreement, while the actual physical time-and-dimensional grids as established by the Universal Physical Laws are, in fact, multi-dimensional and non-chronological. Time is separated on the material worlds through time grids that allow the transition between one layer of reality and the next. These time grids are consistent with the grids located on other planets and stars within your local system and within the Milky Way. The grids separate the layers of realities rather than establish linear time and serve to embed the earth plane with a frequency range that is established by Source at the time of its creation. This frequency range allows Earth's pulse and life patterns to remain coherent with the time grids of the physical universe and the original blueprint of the Local Universe. The multi-dimensional time grid on Earth merges perfectly with an outer boundary – located at 5,000 and 7,000 miles from its circumference – that is *currently* in the shape of a dodecahedron.

---

23   In this case, human incarnation becomes unnecessary for the purpose of mastering karmic debts but remains a voluntary option.

As you travel through the multi-dimensional time grid, you pass from one reality layer to another through an area called "zero point." In order to achieve this reality transfer, the frequency range of each layer must collapse to a zero point before emerging into another dimensional reality. In other words, at each line juncture of this multi-dimensional grid, there exists a zero point – a vortex point – that allows such collapse and transfer. Since Earth's grid is currently in the shape of a dodecahedron, then there is a zero access and transfer point at each juncture of this geometric formation.

THE 32 DIMENSIONS OF THE EARTHLY PLANE ...

There are physical universes, and within each universe and each planetary system there are many layers of reality or "dimensions." As mentioned above, the larger dimensions give birth to the smaller ones, which, in turn, give birth to yet smaller ones and so on and so forth. Conversely, your 32-dimensionality fits within a 96-dimensional reality, which fits within a 288-dimensional reality and this process continues on to infinity, eventually merging all dimensions at the core of your Local Universe, which contains all layers of reality in existence.

As the cosmic light from Source and outer space approaches and collides with the Earth's grid, it fractures like a prism – suddenly creating the illusion of linear Time and Space as separate entities within the earth plane. If we consider a "dimension" to be an aspect of reality, 3-dimensional or otherwise, or a unique experience within the human realm that is within or beyond your 3-dimensional experience, then *there are as many dimensions as can be dictated by the shape or structure in which the universal cosmic light can access the earth plane*. In the case of the Earth, the cosmic light from outer space – which carries information that is absorbed by the human brain and that, in turn, defines reality – is *currently* filtered through the dodecahedron shape of the planetary grid and thus abides by this formation in creating the 32 layers of reality (or dimensions) in existence on the earth plane today.

The dodecahedron is a geometrical shape made of 20 vertices (angles), 12 faces (flat surfaces) and 30 edges. Each vertex holds a specific frequency range that allows a unique experience or access to a layer of reality, while each face creates or gives access to yet another unique dimensional field. This means that there are 32 access points (20 vertices and 12 faces) to a unique experience or layer of reality. Therefore, you may say there are 32 dimensional fields or layers of reality within the earth plane. The reason the 30 edges of the dodecahedron are not taken into account is due to the fact that each edge is part of either a vertex or a face and therefore does not offer a *unique* experience or access to a separate layer of reality.

The current dodecahedron-shaped earth grid also contains other 3-dimensional geometric shapes that include the icosahedron, octahedron, cube and tetrahedron – all together constituting the ensemble reality of the earth plane. Since these 3-dimensional shapes are congruent or contained within each other, their individual vertices, faces or edges do not need to be considered separately as individual reality planes, but rather the juncture point of the different shapes' vertices or the overlap of their faces may be considered as a magnified aspect of the same experience.

DIMENSIONAL ACCESS OF THE DODECAHEDRON

The vertices of the dodecahedron serve to *transfer energy* – in from the cosmos towards the Earth or out from the Earth towards outer space. The faces of the dodecahedron, on the other hand, serve as a *reflective surface* from one area of the Earth to another within the earth plane, or within outer space or between the Earth and space. **See figure 11 on page 44.**

The faces also are openings to other universal unified fields that reflect these alternate realities through a sort of merging or flowing effect, rather than through a thrusting effect such as in the case of the

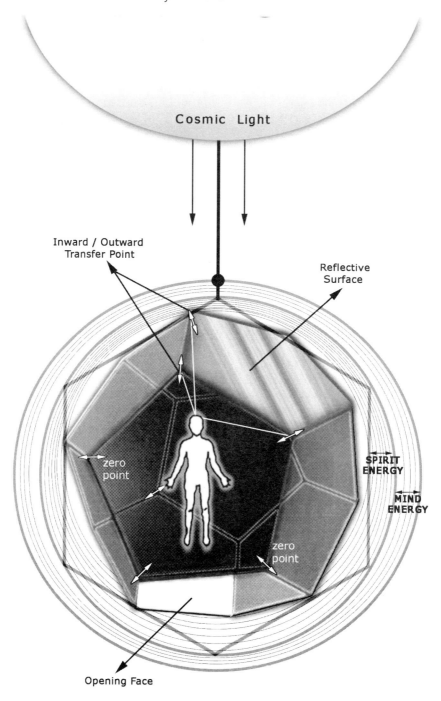

Figure 11: Energy transfer and communication channels within the human energy field.

vertices. Each vertex and face gives access to a specific universal energy that has infinite potential. This means that while one particular vertex point serves to transfer one type of energy from outer space to the heart center of an individual, for example, *the experience of such energy transfer, as it relates to the person experiencing it, is infinite.* No two individual beings may experience the exact same energy transfer in the same way as each being carries his/her own unique chemical, electrical, energetic makeup and own level of consciousness expansion. Similarly, while each face offers access to a specific location or energy point in space, the way this pattern is experienced has infinite potential and is processed by each individual being as a unique event.

32 ACCESS POINTS & DIMENSIONAL EXPERIENCES ...

The 32 dimensional experiences available on the earth plane include access to infinite dimensionality through the doorways provided by the vertices and faces of the dodecahedron. As such, the vertices offer an inward or outward movement – or both – between galactic and cosmic information and the earth plane. This includes cosmic light travel; gravity pull towards the galactic and universal centers; movement of galactic light; spirit and seraphic energy; Mind-Spirit-Physical Energy from the galactic center; Divine Father / Mother / Son energy from Source; Sun and other star energy; fire and volcanic earthly activity; organic or chemical components of the earthly energy; water and oceanic activities; and waste and other disposable earthly energies.

The faces of the dodecahedron, on the other hand, offer the experience of an opening or a reflective panel between Earth and its galactic and universal connections. This includes Divine Father energy; Divine Mother energy; Divine Son energy; Spirit Family[24] energy; outer planetary systems; cosmic light (silver, gold and white); cosmic language; galactic travel; transport grids and systems; and the doorway to Source and the universal center.

---

24 Stream of consciousness comprised of beings in spirit form who share the same lineage.

The 32-dimensional dodecahedron earth grid matches perfectly the human body's first energy field,[25] which also contains all the platonic solids[26] – the tetrahedron, octahedron, cube, and icosahedron – and culminates at the outer most layers of the dodecahedron. The human body thus correlates with the energy field of the current planetary grid in terms of geometric angles, physical proportions, chemical distribution and rotational cycles. This correlation is also found between the human energy field and the planetary grid of other systems as well as the galactic grid and the systems therein.

32-DIMENSIONAL ACCESS AND BRAINWAVE FREQUENCY RANGE ...

Since all energy and divine geometry[27] have resonance and vibration, the 32 layers of reality and their respective access points on the earth plane relate to specific frequency ranges that the human brain may tune into and experience. As you tune into a specific juncture point of the different locations within your energy field – or dodecahedron – you experience the information contained within that point. However, while tuning into the same specific frequency range gives you access to the same information, this information is subject to your individual mind expansion capabilities and results in a subjective experience unique to you. For example, while 1,000Hz is technically associated with the galactic core for one individual, it may only appear or feel like "outer space" to another and may simply feel like cosmic expansion for yet another. **See Chart A on page 47.**

As previously stated, it is impossible to tune precisely into 1,000Hz as you are in continuous motion and no energy is at any time able to be perfectly still. Therefore, as you intend to tune into a unique frequency, you must realize that this frequency is approximate. As such, 1,000Hz is, in fact, ± 1,000Hz and 1KHz is ± 1KHz.

---

[25] **See figure 11 on page 44.**
[26] 3-dimensional aspects of the polygon. All these shapes' sides, edges and angles are congruent.
[27] Geometry based on infinite mathematical numbers, equations, sequences and shapes.

1 GHz	Relates to the universal core and center.
100 KHz	Relates to the distance between all galaxies and the universal center.
10 KHz	Relates to the entire distance between 4 galaxies closest to the Milky Way.
2,000 Hz	Relates to the galactic core adjacent to the Milky Way.
1,500 Hz	Relates to the distance between the Milky Way center and the core of adjacent galaxies.
1,100 Hz	Relates to the fourth and fifth grids encircling the galactic core and the full view of the largest constellation near the center.
1,010 Hz	Relates to the first grid encircling the galactic core.
1,002 Hz	Relates to the radiation around and past the core of the Milky Way.
1,001 Hz	Relates to the radiation around and towards the core of the Milky Way.
1,000 Hz	Relates to the core of the Milky Way.
999 Hz	Relates to a cluster of constellations closest to the galactic core.
998 Hz	Relates to the constellation of Lyra.
997 Hz	Relates to the Pleiades cluster.
996 Hz	Relates to the axial rotation of the galactic core.
995 Hz	Relates to the gravity pull from the Earth towards the galactic core.
994 Hz	Relates to the gravity pull from the galactic core towards the Earth.

CHART A : Examples of approximate frequencies and their equivalent experiences.

You can also experience the various frequencies available through your dimensional makeup by merging consciously the Mind, Spirit and Physical Energies within your heart center and projecting your *intent* into one frequency range at a time. Your intent bypasses the technical aspects described above and transfers your thought into that area of reality at once – producing that which you wish to experience. Such is the process of the human thought and the human mind. Through your intent, however, your experience is once again dependent upon your level of development, which continues to increase and expand until you ultimately realize you have reached the Source from which you have initially originated. This means that you will have come full circle, so to speak, to the original place of your creation that includes all frequencies possible within your intelligent makeup. This process is the awakening of the entire spectrum of frequencies you are made of – from Source to the Earth and from the Earth back to Source. *Mastering this process of awakening your frequency range is the same as the process of awakening to who you really are or what your essence truly is.* This process entails the deliberate activation of your intent with utmost will, precision and control until you come to a full circle of self-realization.

THE NEW EARTH GRID AND THE FUTURE DIMENSIONAL EXPERIENCE ...

As the Earth acquires a new cosmic position,[28] the human body also adjusts to its new frequency range and resonance. As such, the human brain automatically opens up to new energy forms unable to be retrieved on Earth up until this time. Such an occurrence results from the expiration of the old cells, so to speak, that correlated specifically with the patterns instilled by the current grid position and its limitations. The reason for the termination of the current earth grid shape and position is that it does not comply with the intelligent design or divine blueprint with which the grid structure and harmonics were originally created. Such geometric forms as the platonic shapes – which include the dodecahedron – are based on the polyhedron, which is a mathematically finite number. While physi-

---

28 Details are described in later chapters.

cal reality *appears* material and somewhat inanimate due its cellular slower motion, speed and rotation cycles, it is nevertheless created and instilled by Physical Energy, or the Divine Son aspect of Source, which is *infinite*. The base of all life, including physical life, is continuous motion, continuous self-regeneration, self-management and self-sustenance. The fact that physical life appears otherwise to the human eye does not deny the truth and absolute fact of its perpetual self-regenerating nature. The dodecahedron of the earth grid, which is a finite configuration, has created a reality – and all the manifested forms therein – that is false, invented or man-made and is unsupported by the cosmic laws. This means that life on Earth as you know it has complied for millennia with an energetic form and principles *unrecognized by the infinite Laws of Creation* and, therefore, does not exist! The life on Earth that you know is indeed an illusory reality that must eventually be mended and restored to its original divine blueprint.

As of the tremendous cosmic shift that completes in 2012, however, the earth grid positions the planet in a new divine geometric alignment with the galactic center, suddenly opening the doorways to infinite dimensionality and potential. The new earth grid will appear as a continuous formation of *hexagonal shapes* within a holographic sphere covering the circumference of the planet at the approximate same location of 5,000 to 7,000 miles. This movement and shift alter the amount of cosmic light that reaches the Earth and the way by which this light is experienced by the individual. Rather than observing one octave of light waves and frequencies as before the shift, the human brain is now able to absorb, through the pineal gland, 2 or more octaves of light – depending on the individual's level of consciousness and development.

Currently, when the cosmic light bends as it refracts against the earth grid, this light is absorbed by the pineal gland and the physical brain in such a way so as to create the illusion of 3 dimensions. However, when this light bending is altered through the new earth shifts, the pineal gland creates a new receptor, so to speak, to accommodate the added light octaves – thus producing an additional dimensional experience. The new earth grid will then allow access to all points within the galaxy and the universe, transforming the current human experience drastically from a limited 32-dimensional access field to infinite potentiality. The synchronicity of the Earth's grid movement with the geophysical adjustments and the transmutation of the human brain make this transition a natural and gradual experience, lasting a period of approximately 13 years – from the year 2,000 to 2013 – until the Earth is settled into a new position in perfect alignment with Source.

The divine geometrical formation of the hexagons corresponds to the density and pulse of the new planet being born. As the shift happens, the correlation between the Earth's pulse, rotational axis and other atmospheric adjustments allows this new hexagonal formation to be implemented, not only on Earth but for the entire solar system. These hexagonal shapes are not only based on divine geometry by nature but are a new vibration altogether, a frequency range that allows the filtration of cosmic light from Source to be absorbed on the entire planet *evenly*. Up until 2,000 years ago, several crucial axes responsible for transferring cosmic light homogeneously throughout your planetary system had been dismantled and some even destroyed. These axes are part of the planetary grid and are responsible for implanting information within specific areas of the Earth's surface so as to replenish the planet with the ingredients necessary for perpetual renewable energy and growth. When these systems were tampered with, such vital life energy ceased to reach certain areas of the planet and triggered energetic starvation. The long-drawn chaos observed in various parts of the planet – namely in Asia, Africa and the Mid-East – is the direct consequence of the interruption of cosmic flow within these regions. However, as of 2012, the reparation of the various dismantled axes is complete and the emergence of the new hexagonal grid structure allows, through the process of universal reflectivity, the projection of an even and consistent solar and cosmic frequency range throughout the globe. When such a system is implemented within the entire solar system, your Earth automatically opens up to the intelligence and energetic information present on those other planets without the need for artificial satellite transmission. Your solar system then becomes one cohesive creation fitting perfectly within the formation of the yet larger scope of your galaxy. As such, the Milky Way will also be adjusting its parameters in such a way so as to implement this tremendous change and perfectly integrate this change within the cosmic order.

The hexagonal divine geometry of your new planet allows a new vibration to be transposed from one point of the universe to another faster than the speed of light without the need for human technology. Since Earth's new divine geometry is based on the universal principles of golden ratios and infinite formulas, it now fits perfectly within the plan of the entire cosmos and begins to interact spontaneously with all access points of the galaxy and, in turn, the universe by matching all zero-point locations present in the cosmos. The actual alignment of these zero points is currently taking place and it is at the completion of such movement that the Earth, along with its neighboring planets, will lock itself into its new position and alignment and will create a brilliant and coherent cosmic interaction. Once achieved, the new positioning of the planet and solar system begins to interact spontaneously with other realities through electromagnetic transmutation, transferring the energy each world is blasting into a form of energy that is spontaneously assimilated and understood on other worlds. Such a process is inherent and encoded within all Physical Energy creation, interaction and universal bonding.

HUMAN INCARNATION AND PARALLEL EXISTENCE ...

Once you have agreed to incarnate in human form, you assign a portion of your consciousness into the time / space continuum and reality you have agreed to partake in – Earth – while leaving the core of your true essence at your location of origin. For example, those beings originating from another star system continue existing in that star system while one portion of their essence and consciousness simultaneously appears on Earth in the body of a human. This simultaneous existence is not considered a "past life" – but rather "parallel" – since the projection of consciousness occurs through the zero point transfer access of the inter-galactic grids and thus transcends the time / space continuum.

You may also choose to incarnate in human form at several intervals within the human time / space continuum, in other words, within Earth's chronological history. In this case, the aspect of your being that is projected from your star system into the human realm at 500 AD for example, continues to reappear in 1200 AD, 1600 AD, 2000 AD and so on and so forth. This form of existence, while seemingly chronological and intermittent from a human perspective is, in fact, simultaneous or parallel from the viewpoint of your original essence and consciousness that have initiated at once such a life cycle. What is recognized as "reincarnation" or "past lives" on your world is nothing but a creative process that allows your consciousness to achieve one unique purpose through several *seemingly* consecutive appearances.

It can also occur that your consciousness is great enough that you are able to occupy the body of 2 or 3 humans at once within the same time / space continuum. In this case, your original essence and consciousness remain anchored in its original abode and projects a larger portion of itself within the human realm. This form of simultaneous existence is also considered parallel existence, since all 3 humans are you, co-existing within the same time / space continuum while holding 3 separate identities or residing in different locations.

Moreover, it is indeed possible to experience all 3 ways of parallel existence at once. You may be aware of your individual self in your current human body while having been present on the Earth for the past 2000 years, for example, in other bodies or identities performing similar tasks. Simultaneously, other forms of yourself may also be in parallel bodies on the earth plane, while yet other aspects of your being may be in transition as well as present in your original star system all at once. As such, there is an infinite number of ways to manifest as parallel identities simultaneously on various worlds and no 2 beings have the exact same configuration of parallel lives.

PARALLEL EXISTENCE AND THE DIVINE PLAN …

Through parallel existence, the more massive consciousnesses – such as the Divine Masters' and the Divine Sons' among many others – are able to de-particularize and exist simultaneously within the earth plane and beyond. In order to succeed in their pre-determined mission on Earth, they create a deliberate web of energy particles that encompasses all reality aspects and possible doorways as they station themselves at the propitious locations of that web. Through their earthly awakening, such Divine Beings reassemble, so to speak, the memory of their dispersed aspects, thereby igniting the respective energetic charge of each aspect. Once all aspects of their manifested selves are activated, the web of that massive consciousness creates a new vibration and thus a new reality on its own that others may attach themselves onto. These others may then begin to create their reality according to the newly manifested divine configuration. Such process takes a tremendous amount of energy focus on the part of the Divine Being in human form as it accelerates the momentum of reality creation for their aspect in human form as well as the entire humanity all at once. The awakening and activation of the dispersed aspects of the Divine Beings' web is the very process by which the new earth grid configuration is created and manifested. In other words, the awakening of these Divine Beings in human form to their parallel aspects is simultaneous with and responsible for the birth of the new grid and future reality on the earth plane. **See figure 12 on page 54.**

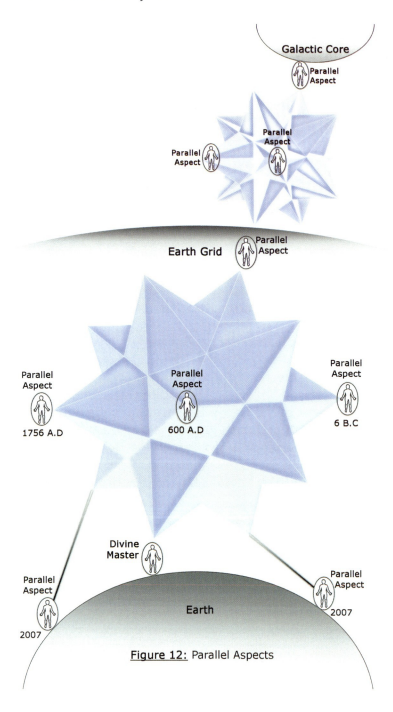

Figure 12: Parallel Aspects

Note

The following chapter serves to describe the universal order that is integrated within the Local Universe and those aspects that are most relevant to humanity's evolution and progress. It is truly impossible to describe such concepts as divine creation, divine organization and cosmic intelligent design in a pure and truthful manner through the use of a limited human language. I will, therefore, attempt to use the most appropriate terms available in the English language to depict such tremendously complex outer-worldly concepts. At no time do the words "government," "supervise," "administrators," "supreme council" or "hierarchy," to only name a few, refer to the typically recognized human concepts. Such terms are simply used to offer a general representation of the extraordinary multi-faceted Cosmic and Divine Orders. You may also liken the organization of the Divine Orders, as described herein, as *one body* in which each system or organ is uniquely configured to perform a specified duty. This particular system or organ, however, cannot be regarded as an entity separate from the main organism or the *One Consciousness* that created it.

4

Creation Of Your Local Universe:

The Invisible Government

Prior to the implanting of intelligent life within your Local Universe, the Power Controllers and Life Architects[29] of the Central Universe create a nebula-like fabric out of the multi-universal structure already in existence and transport this replicated formula into the new environment. The new nebula remains dormant for a period of time until it becomes amply charged with adequate life properties and creates sufficient heat necessary to ignite the atomic elements contained within it. The ignition of atomic elements creates a chain reaction, so to speak, and propels the nebula's core into an enormous nuclear blast. The dispersed nebula particles then spread throughout space according to their pre-established type and properties. This means that the very composition of the nebula's particles has an inherent shape or configuration, rotation and speed that allows them to travel through space according to these attributes. Once the particles achieve their first course through space, the universal core pulls them back into its orbit until they stabilize in a primal position

---

29   Beings of the highest Creator Order who are in charge of producing new life forms and implanting them on the various worlds.

and become integrated within the space breathing patterns already present in the universe. This gradual assimilation into the universal breathing is established by the omnipresent Spirit Energy that seamlessly incorporates the new nebula particles fully within the rhythm of the whole. The rate of space expansion and retraction depends upon the pre-established properties of a given universe. In your universe, space breathing occurs at the rate of 500,000 years per inhalation or exhalation. Through space breathing, the individual particles of the nebula then continue to expand and retract, continuously interacting with yet new forms of energy and forming new clusters with respective orbits. These individual particles and clusters are the planets, solar systems and galaxies that you observe today.

Once the planets, constellations and galaxies arrive at a somewhat stable condition, the right "arm" of the Divine Father – Mind Energy – expands from the universal core and circulates throughout space in a counterclockwise-like motion while a left "arm" – also from the Divine Father – travels clockwise.[30] Both "arms" become perfectly merged and upheld by the unifying energy of the Divine Mother, or Spirit Energy. These colossal energetic arms and gravitational motions spring from the universal core with massive force and begin to pour repetitively into each galactic center being created for an average period of 1 million years – until each galaxy forms its own disk-like shape. Once this formation has been achieved, it is then spun into one rotational direction or another. In the case of the Milky Way, the rotational movement has been clockwise-like for approximately 5 billion years as observed from the universal center. It will begin, however, to suspend its current course and establish a new motion, matching the new energies being instilled within its core. This shift in rotational galactic movement is responsible for the intermittent adjustments in solar calibration and the subsequent polar shifts observed on the individual planets.

PROPERTIES OF A GALAXY ...

Once the galaxies are formed, the individual planets and solar systems within them begin to take form and stabilize their unique

---

30 As perceived from the perspective of Source. It is, however, a simplistic way to describe the very complex and unique movement of this energy.

orbits and axis rotation. The galactic structure matches perfectly the fabric of the original nebula with which it was created as well as a new form of energy that is particular to that galaxy. While all galaxies within your Local Universe follow similar creation patterns and organization, the energy forms *within* your galaxy are not identical to others present in your universe. Galaxies form a different energetic and electromagnetic pattern as they rotate around the core of the universe and around each other. Each galaxy eventually settles into its own unique energetic formation yet remains cohesive with all other galaxies in existence as well as the universal core.

The energy forms within the Milky Way include the currently observed physical, chemical, and electromagnetic forms and also the universal forms of energies, such as Mind and Spirit, which are indiscernible through the physical instruments currently in use by your scientists. While the *effects* of Mind and Spirit and some aspects of Physical Energies are detectable within your worlds, these energies cannot be measured accurately unless they are pre-supposed to be in existence and understood in terms of a universal *Mind* – a multi-faceted, multi-dimensional infinite Energy Source and *Being*. Similarly, the energy forms in other galaxies are also immeasurable through the current human instruments since the very essence of Source creation is still poorly understood.

CREATION OF INTELLIGENT BEINGS WITHIN YOUR LOCAL UNIVERSE ...

Prior to the arrival of the Divine Father and Divine Mother upon a new world, the Power Controllers and Life Architects maneuver energy within the outer space in such a way as to begin shaping planets, stars and universes that can sustain a new form of life. Upon the completion of such a brilliant and complex task, the Creators of the new worlds appear and the creation of intelligent life is then envisioned, carefully designed and brilliantly implemented. Your Local Universe follows similar preparation, organization and creative principles.

THE DIVINE FATHER ...

The Divine Father of your Local Universe is the embodiment of the Universal Mind / Father and the Universal Body / Son of the Creator-Source. He is the first-born of Creation and is of the *Descending Order of Creators* capable of carrying and representing the Universal Father / Mind and Universal Son / Body in different aspects and capacity within the Local Universe. *Your Divine Father is the Mind Energy of your Local Universe.* Also, He is the original Creator as well as the visionary, inventor, director and administrator of your entire universe, which includes countless galaxies, constellations and habitable and non-habitable[31] planets and stars. The Divine Father is also Time and Space reality, which means He defines Time and Space and can suspend them both at will and upon command. He is the most brilliant Being within your universe and the only One in charge of restoring order within a system that has been quarantined by continuous destructive energy. For the purpose of such unique bestowals,[32] He creates and directs a remarkable plan formerly approved by the Universal Father / Son and the Divine Assembly of the Central Universe.

THE DIVINE SON ...

Once your Divine Father takes jurisdiction over the Local Universe of His creation, He is able to integrate within the physical realms He creates through the energy of the Divine Son or the physical aspect of His personality. This Divine Son is the 4th of the 7 possible aspects of the First Source of your Local Universe. **See figure 13 on page 61.**

The Divine Son is the Physical Energy of your Local Universe. Also, He is Space Reality, which means he defines and can suspend Space – but not Time – at will and upon command when incarnated in human form.[33]

---

31 These planets are not yet ready to be inhabited.
32 Dispensations.
33 He can be everywhere at once.

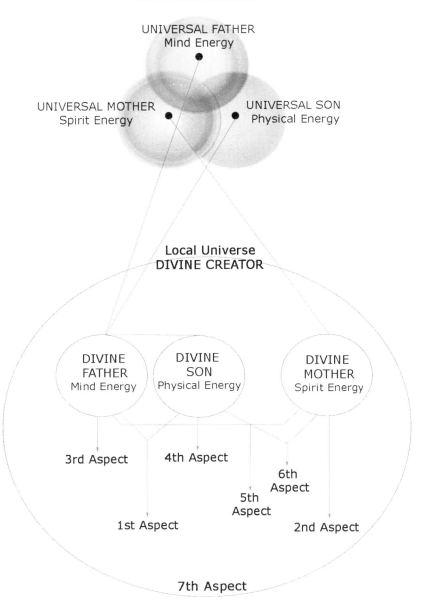

Figure 13: The 7 aspects of the Divine Creator of the Local Universe.

The Divine Sons of a Local Universe, also recognized as the descending Sons of God, are categorized by order: the First Order of Divine Sons carry the largest mass of consciousness and are able to conduct and master universal affairs; the Second Order of Divine Sons master and control galactic affairs; the Third Order of Divine Sons master and manage the planetary system affairs. For example, the Planetary Supervisor of your planet is a Divine Son – or Son of God – of the Third Order. While He is nonetheless of the Divine and Creator Orders, He is able to bring His vibration in close proximity to the material beings, thus becoming the most appropriate type of Divine Sons for such post.

The Divine Father of the Local Universe is embodied and manifested in the material worlds at first through the Divine Son of the First Order. And as there are 7 possible aspects of the First Source, this manifested Divine Son becomes all 7 aspects of this First Source through each incarnation and may subsequently represent one or more of these 7 aspects each time He manifests in material form. Or, you may say, that this Divine Son of the First Order may manifest 1 aspect of Source through each incarnation, human or otherwise. Once this magnificent Being has completed the 7 possible deity manifestations, He becomes a 7-aspect Divine Son.

This 7-aspect Divine Son is responsible for representing and implanting the original principles of the First Source – The Divine Father / Mother – which are: Omnipotence, Omnipresence, Omniscience, Love, Truth, Beauty and Goodness. These principles become personalized through His 7 consecutive incarnations that allow the integration of such principles within the earth plane or other realms. The incarnations of the 7-aspect Divine Sons of the First Order are thus the process through which the energy of the Divine Creator becomes permanently implanted on a new world. **See figure 14 on page 63.**

Once the 7-aspect Divine Son has manifested all principles of the First Source, He then allows the fragmentation[34] of His consciousness within the worlds He has occupied. Each time a particle of His being that He leaves behind on a given world repeats itself, so to speak, it creates a separate and new identity with each incarnation or fragmentation. Since there are 7 aspects for His *original* fragment, there will be 336 ways to carry further these respective principles through

---

34 Deliberate de-particularization.

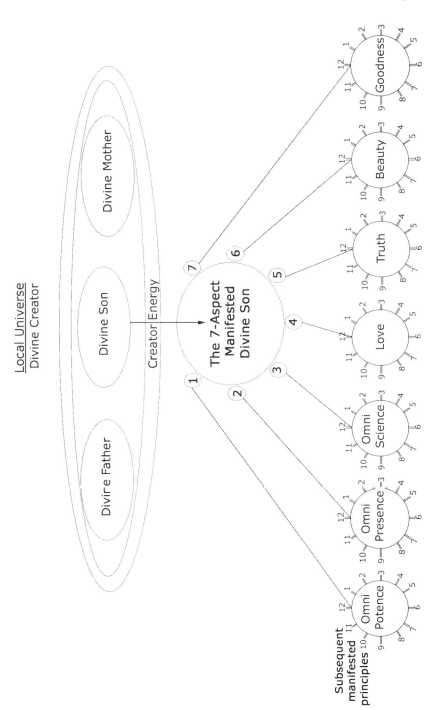

Figure 14: The 7 Manifested Principles of the 7-Aspect Divine Son and subsequent manifestations.

various combinations with individual identities. As such, there can be 49 combinations of 1-principle Divine Sons, 72 combinations of 2-principle Divine Sons, 75 combinations of 3-principle Divine Sons, 64 combinations of 4-principle Divine Sons, 45 combinations of 5-principle Divine Sons, 24 combinations of 6-principle Divine Sons and 7 combination of all 7-principle Divine Sons.

On the earth plane, such a brilliant regeneration process has been realized through the manifestation of the Divine Father in the body of various Divine Sons and Masters such as Buddha, Krishna, Mohammed or the Master Jesus to only name a few. However, it is at the completion of the Master Jesus' extraordinary appearance that a particle of the Divine Father's original configuration, present in the human body of this Master, remained on the earth plane. This Divine Father entity then de-particularized 110 times and subsequently 1,100 times through what appears to you as separate incarnations. Each of these 1,100 particles carries the same original formula or frequency range and yet allows each to become its own unique and newly-formed identity or personality. This means that, while all humans carry the divine DNA within them, there are 1,100 individual beings carrying the original Divine Father formula – as this formula was manifested on the earth plane 2,000 years ago – in one form or another, in one capacity or another. Since not all 1,100 are able to carry the original Divine Father formula in precisely the exact same capacity, these 1,100 particles are not equal in consciousness, mass and power. Therefore, at present, each of these particle reflects, carries or embodies one or more principles of the Divine Father on the Earth.

THE DIVINE MOTHER ...

The Divine Mother of your Local Universe is the embodiment of the Universal Spirit of the Creator-Source. She is the original co-Creator of your entire universe, which includes countless galaxies, constellations and habitable and non-habitable planets and stars. *The Divine Mother is the Spirit Energy of your Local Universe.* She functions as the life force, so to speak, that filters and breathes through all intelligent beings and the physical worlds. She is the ultimate creative partner and sublime nurturer of all forms of life within your universe. The Divine Mother is the breath and pulse of your space or the energy that sustains the perpetual breathing and pulsation of each planetary and solar system, each galaxy and the far-flung universe all at once. Finally, the Divine Mother is Time Reality, which means She defines and can suspend Time, but not space, at will and upon command.

THE INVISIBLE GOVERNMENT OF YOUR LOCAL UNIVERSE ...

Once the physical universe has been created, the Divine Father and Mother of your Local Universe bring forth the first intelligent being: the *Chief Executive* in charge of the overall administration of the universe. This brilliant Being is the true governor and overseer of multitudinous tasks that include creating and managing the judicial and legislative[35] systems of your universe in addition to being the chief advisor and prime minister to the Divine Father. While the Chief Executive is the first created intelligent being of your Local Universe, He is considered a "brother" in relation to the Divine Son rather than a first-born son. He remains closely attached to the Divine Father's affairs and replaces Him in times of need or planetary bestowals. The Chief Executive heads the *Supreme Council,* which comprises 1,000 members from the various galaxies and planetary systems.

The 1,000 members of the *Supreme Council* in the Local Universe are in charge of all judicial matters of the universe. This council organizes the election and appointment of the various Divine Sons and Universal Aids to myriad posts. This Council has supreme authority in all matters of universal imbalance and disturbance and represents your Local Universe within the court conglomerations at the Central Universe.

The *Archangels* are created through the mind of the Divine Father and Mother. These powerful beings minister to the intelligent beings inhabiting the various worlds. They create harmony and peace and

---

35   Not to be confused with the human judicial and legislative systems.

allow freedom to prevail. When disrupting upheaval occurs within a newly-formed material world, the Archangels are the beings who defend the oppressed creatures and their territories, so to speak, in order to sustain the energetic harmony between the worlds. They are supervised by the Chief Executive, who is in charge of the seraphic[36] and other orders that oversee the safe emancipation of the material worlds.

The Melchizedeks constitute one of the highest orders of Creation and are typically magnificent teachers within the material realms. They are created from the energy of the Divine Father and embody His divine energy within your universe. These divine creatures are called by the order of the First Melchizedek and the Divine Father of the Central Universe to assist a world in disarray. These beings normally dwell within your world in spirit form but may occasionally incarnate to aid the spiritual advancement of your species.

The *Galactic Administrators* are of the second Creator Order – or Divine Sons of the Second Order – and are created for the purpose of governing and overseeing the multitudinous galaxies. Their prime work is to calibrate the different systems within their respective galaxies according to the universal government's laws. These Divine Sons report to the Chief Executive and the Supreme Court all matters related to universal organization.

The planetary and solar systems are governed by the *System Administrators*. These brilliant beings are Divine Sons of the Third Order and are in charge of materializing the energy control and distribution needs of their respective planetary or solar systems. They report to their individual Galactic Administrators and remain in close communication with each *Planetary Supervisor* within their system.

Each inhabited planet is governed by a *Planetary Supervisor*. This Being and part of His court sit at the apex of the planetary grid. He is in charge of maintaining energetic balance between his planet and its neighboring worlds. The Planetary Supervisor is of the 3rd Divine Sons Order and is closest to the evolutionary[37] and material beings in terms of consciousness. He is also responsible for monitoring the outburst of harmful energy. If such destructive patterns become so great as to threaten the original divine blueprint of the planet, the

---

36 Angelic.
37 Type of beings who need to incarnate in material form in order to expand their consciousness. Humans are evolutionary beings.

Planetary Supervisor requests indemnity from the System Administrator who assesses the gravity of the matter and dispatches supporting agents accordingly. If the destructive energy becomes uncontainable, the Planetary Supervisor and the respective System Administrator are obligated to surrender their sovereignty to the Chief Executive and the Supreme Court for such unique affairs. In the case of your Earth, it was the Chief Executive and subsequently the Divine Father himself who intervened 2,000 years ago to halt the escalating momentum of damage and destruction. While you may still perceive the remnant surges of human evil and selfishness, the *underlying causes* of this destructive energy have been annihilated indeed, and long-lasting peace will soon begin to surface on your planet.

The invisible universal government is your commanding celestial body in charge of eradicating the chaos, anguish and tremendous suffering that have plagued your world for millennia. You must realize that such a plan cannot fail as the will of the Divine Creator is final and absolute. While human free will on your planet is still being led by poor judgment, material futility and extreme selfishness, it is now the Divine Father's will to reverse the damage incurred thus far and restore His permanent link with His beloved children of Time and Space. **See figure 15 on page 68.**

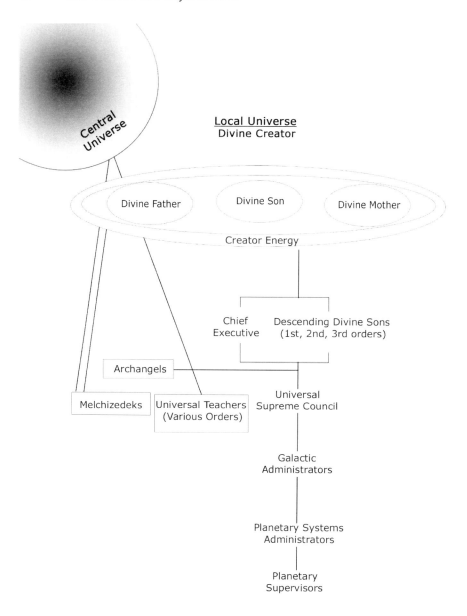

Figure 15: The invisible universal government of the Local Universe

Note

While the term "Source" generally refers to the Creator-Source who is the original Creator of all life, as well as the actual location of the First Center of Creation, I will use the terms "Source" and "First Center" to also refer to the Divine Creator and the core of this Local Universe. Since the energy of the Creator-Source is replicated in the beings as well as the centers of all the universes, the term Source can be used for all universes interchangeably. In the following pages, however, Source will refer to the Creator and the First Center of this Local Universe for the information transcribed herein pertains to the Earth, the Milky Way and this Local Universe.

Part II

Unfolding The Divine Plan

5

The Intelligent Beings Involved In The Divine Plan

It is a difficult task to describe the countless number of intelligent beings in existence on Earth and within your galaxy, some of whom are simply indescribable in human terms. So, we shall describe those who are pertinent to your species' awakening and planetary evolution through the transition of 2012.

Similar to mind-al, spiritual and physical energy, intelligent beings – visible and invisible – interact with you on a conscious or unconscious level. On Earth, all beings create – through thought – their individual reality and experience while at the same time contributing to the collective human experience through energetic exchange. Regardless of your particular location on Earth, you, as an individual soul, are contributing to the overall human experience of others by the very fact that, through physical incarnation, all beings belong to the same human mind matrix. *Each time one individual thinks, s/he influences the outcome of the global human experience. This is a fact and universal law.* The current planetary shift is therefore being created by you, individually and collectively, as we speak. However, while there are myriad types of beings co-existing with you on Earth, *it is only those who are in human form who can directly affect the outcome of the human collective mind matrix.* This is why many beings who are typically not required to incarnate in physical form have chosen the human experience at this moment in time – to integrate with and affect the outcome of human thought. Those in spirit form, or other invisible physical beings,[38] can *influence* the mind of humans but may *not directly affect* humanity's outcome. Therefore, an understanding of the beings currently in existence on Earth – visible or invisible – helps create a realistic and truthful picture of how the current individual human mind may be affecting the collective matrix and creating the planetary evolution outcome of 2012.

INTELLIGENT BEINGS INVOLVED IN THE DIVINE PLAN ...

The Divine Plan consists of an uplifting or shifting process that tilts planet Earth and your planetary system in such a way as to re-establish the mind-al, spiritual and physical circuit alignment with Source. The Divine Plan is multi-dimensional, occurring on myriad aspects and layers of reality at once. It is initiated by your Divine Creators, Divine Sons and the Divine Assembly in conjunction with Celestial Agencies, Universal Beings, various types of Light and Star Beings and Galactic Citizens as well as Human and other Physical Beings of the highest order. All are working in unison to instill this magnificent and elaborate plan to anchor *the divine principles* within the human plane. **See Figure 16 on page 75.**

THE DIVINE PRINCIPLES IN HUMAN FORM ...

Prior to implanting the divine principles within the newly-created worlds, the Divine Father first instills the various aspects of the Creator-Source upon each planet of His universe. Throughout the history of your Local Universe, the Divine Father has already manifested the 7 aspects of the Creator-Source on various worlds, including the Earth. The first manifestation represented the 7th aspect of the Creator-Source (the Universal Father / Son / Spirit). The second manifestation represented the 6th aspect of the Creator-Source (the Universal Son / Spirit). The third manifestation represented the 5th aspect of

---

38 Beings from other planetary systems who inhabit the earth plane but exist in another layer of reality (frequency range) and thereby remain invisible to the human eye.

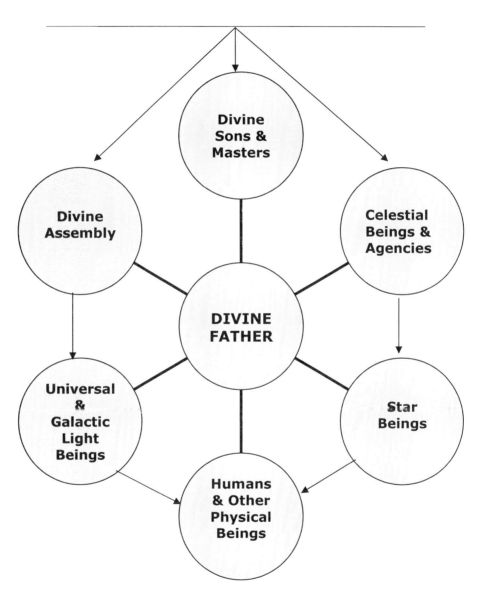

Figure 16: The Divine Plan on Earth is lead by the Divine Sons and Masters but it involves many other universal, celestial, galactic, star, human and other physical beings.

the Creator-Source (the Universal Father / Spirit). The fourth manifestation represented the 4th aspect of the Creator-Source (the Universal Father / Son). The fifth manifestation represented the 3rd aspect of the Creator-Source (the Universal Spirit). The sixth manifestation represented the 2nd aspect of the Creator-Source (the Universal Son) and the 7th manifestation represented the 1st aspect of the Creator-Source (the Universal Father). **See figure 17 on page 77.**

Your Divine Father is therefore a *7-aspect Creator-Son* and He continues to integrate Himself in human form through the subsequent incarnation of His Divine Sons and other Masters of various orders. These incarnated Sons represent the *divine principles* of the First Source (Divine Father / Mother), which are: Omnipotence, Omnipresence, Omniscience, Love, Truth, Beauty and Goodness. These 7 main principles are now reflected, carried and embodied by the Divine Sons, Masters and all other beings involved in the Divine Plan of 2012 on the earth plane. Each principle characterizes a specific energy form or vibration of Source. It is a difficult task to accurately describe these individual principles in a language that you may comprehend, as the very creative formula of these beings and principles is non-human and is unrecognized by the human brain. Therefore, we shall attempt to describe the process through which these 7 divine principles are embodied and brought into your worlds in the physical appearance of the Divine Sons, Divine Masters and many other magnificent universe personalities.

The *First Divine Son* embodies the *Omnipotence* principle of the Divine Father, which is the administrative and managerial attributes of the Divine Father and Son. At Source, it is the Divine Father who creates intelligent life within the universe but it is the Divine Son who manages the actual organization and administration of the worlds. This attribute of the Divine Son is the energy that allows you to experience universal order and the inherent intelligence of life. When a Divine Son embodies such a divine principle in human form, He tends to specialize in the area of government, global management or politics. While His daily work may appear to consist of the organization of state matters, for example, His true energetic work involves the implementation of the universal governmental structure and principles within the earth plane for the purpose of maintaining

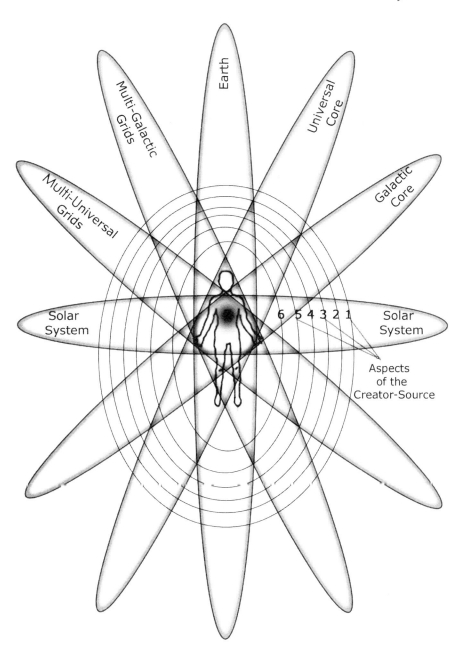

Figure 17: The 7- aspect Divine Son manifested on Earth

communication, evolution and balance within the galactic structure and, subsequently, with the core of the universe.

The *Second Divine Son* embodies the *Omnipresence* principle of the Divine Father, which is the gravitational pull of all intelligent life towards the First Center – the core of the Local Universe. Omnipresence is a force or energy that is based on one divine blueprint, allowing the life experience to be interactive, interrelated and interconnected. The magnetic pull you experience regarding understanding, knowing and merging with your Creator is due to this magnificent gravitational energy that emanates from the Divine Son and that provides unity within the universe. When a Divine Son embodies such a divine principle in human form, He tends to specialize in the area of electromagnetic planetary healing and other energy and gravity manipulation. While His apparent work may consist of healing or teaching spiritual truths, His true energetic work involves the maneuvering of tremendous gravitational circuits within the earth plane and the galactic core and subsequently the core of the universe.

The *Third Divine Son* embodies the *Omniscience* principle of the Divine Father, which includes the energy of wisdom, reason and all-knowingness. This Divine Son carries within His very being the ability to know all that is at any moment in time. The inherent intelligent design and mechanism of all life stem from this divine principle of all-knowingness of Source. When a Divine Son embodies such a divine principle in human form, He tends to specialize in the area of science, mathematics or philosophy. While His apparent work may include technology, scientific research and inventions, for example, His energetic work involves the opening of Mind Energy channels between the collective human mind matrix and the galactic and universal cores. This process enables the human mind to absorb higher information and universal knowledge that contribute to its evolution and expansion.

The *Fourth Divine Son* embodies the *Love* principle of the Divine Father / Mother, which can be described as a multi-universal experience that is bound in one seamless intelligence or fabric. It is this energy that creates the principle of oneness on a cosmic level and attracts similar vibrations unto itself in a constant and perpetual manner. In human terms, this principle is the feeling of utter inner joy that resonates with Life and Creation itself. When a Divine Son embodies such a divine principle in human form, He tends to specialize in the area of spiritual teaching, healing and social service. While His apparent work may range from human rights activism and philanthropy to selfless healing practices, His energetic work consists of anchoring the Love principle of Creation into the very blueprint of the planet, the human body, mind and spirit. Such individuals also work closely with the various species within the earth plane such as the animal species and the plant life for the purpose of elevating their respective consciousness and blending them more fully with the cosmic intelligent design.

The *Fifth Divine Son* embodies the *Truth* principle of Source, which is the transparent aspect of the creative principles embedded in the being of the Divine Mother. It is the aspect that allows all intelligent life to see and experience the divinity of Source, embody that divinity fully and completely and utilize it to create reality. When a Divine Son embodies such a divine principle in human form, He tends to specialize in the area of education, philosophy and spiritual teaching. His energetic work, however, includes re-establishing the communication grids and axes within the earth plane and the galaxy, sustaining the energy and vibrations of Source within the ruling organizations on the planet and allowing cosmic communication to flow within the earth plane.

The *Sixth Divine Son* embodies the *Beauty* principle of Source, which is defined as the divine geometry, symmetry, rhythm and movement embedded in the being of the Divine Mother. These elegant attributes perpetuate a sense of harmony and homogeny throughout Creation. This principle is represented as beauty in physical reality but it is more of a spiritual or essential quality rather than a visual and finite experience. When a Divine Son embodies such a divine principle in human form, He tends to specialize in the area of art, social and cultural activities. However, His energetic work involves bringing forth evolved formulas, divine geometry and intricate designs from various parts of the galaxy and beyond.

The *Seventh Divine Son* embodies the *Goodness* principle embedded in the being of the Divine Mother, which is the inherent desire to maintain the original principles and blueprint of Creation and

Divinity. Goodness at Source is one aspect of the Divine Mother that permeates through all intelligent life and blends into one binding and harmonious energy. In human terms, goodness is simply the desire to do good and display love and morality towards others as well as bestow it onto one's self. When a Divine Son embodies such a divine principle in human form, He tends to specialize in the area of social service or ethnic and spiritual services. However, His energetic work consists of instilling the Divine Mother vibration where it is most needed on the earth plane. This process helps elevate humanity's consciousness to blend more cohesively with the galactic and universal communities.

While the 7 Divine Sons are the first beings to instill the principles of the Divine Creator on a material world, they may also represent one or more principle in subsequent incarnations or a different principle from one incarnation to the next. Such is also the process for other Divine Masters – those of the Ascended Order – as well as the Light, Celestial and other Universal Beings who collaborate, to a lesser degree, in the manifestation of these principles in human form. While one Divine Son represents in human form the Omniscience principle and the Mind Energy of the Divine Father, He may be working intimately with the mind channels of the entire humanity and reestablishing their mind-al link with Source. Simultaneously, another Divine Master of the Ascended Order, for example, may represent the Goodness and Love principles and enhance humanity's moral and selfless values. Yet another Light Being of the Galactic Federation may be representing the Beauty principle of Source, bringing forth new brilliant divine geometry patterns that inspire and uplift the human spirit. Together and through their own specialization, so to speak, these conscious Divine Masters begin to manifest a multi-dimensional sublime experience that uplifts all levels of humanity and Earth's consciousness into one cohesive and magnificent evolutionary species. **See figure 14 on page 63**.

THE PROCESS OF MANIFESTING THE DIVINE PRINCIPLES IN HUMAN FORM …

The processes by which the Divine Sons and Masters appear on your worlds occur in various ways and include several steps. Throughout the human incarnation, the Divine Son begins by *representing* the divine principle He carries through telepathic contact with the Spirit Family. This process occurs through the *reflectivity* of the energy from Source into the physical realm with the help of the Spirit Family. The connection remains somewhat outside the self rather than becoming integrated as one physical and divine energy. This process of representation – through reflectivity – is then followed by the actual *carrying* of the divine aspect He represents, which entails a merged or blended experience of both the energies of Source and the physical body. This process may be intermittent throughout the physical life of the Divine Son on Earth or begin at a certain point of His career and remain integrated within His physical energy for the remainder of the physical incarnation. Finally, the carrying process is followed by the actual and full *embodiment* of the divine principle and aspect in question. This process typically occurs at a specific point in the Masters' physical life and remains integrated within His being until the end of the earthly incarnation. **See figure 18 on page 82.**

THE INCARNATION PROCESS OF THE DIVINE SON …

The actual incarnation process of the Divine Son may happen in of the following ways:

1. The Divine Son appears already in the form of an adult human, in full recollection of His true divine essence. This manner of infiltrating the human reality is extremely rare and may no longer be required at this stage of evolution on Earth.

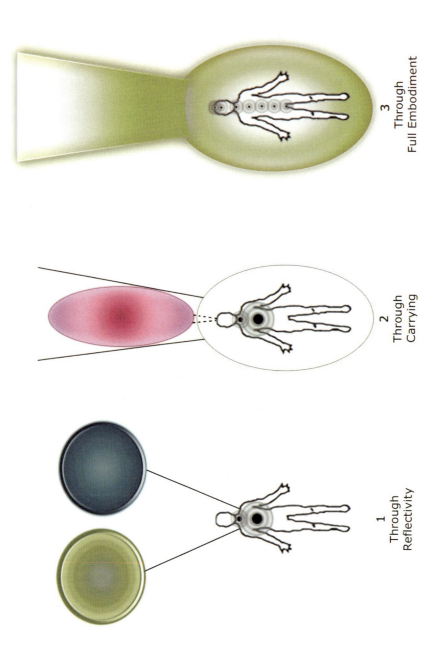

Figure 18: Process of manifesting the Divine Principles in human form

2. The Divine Son appears as a human infant through natural birth and gradually awakens to His true essence. He needs to recollect only enough information to allow Him to perform His divine duties with full consciousness and deliberate intent. His representation of the Creator Energy,[39] the Divine Father and Mother, is partial – either through reflectivity, the carrying process or through partial embodiment.
3. The Divine Son appears as a human infant without the experience of natural birth. He needs to recollect at first only enough information to allow Him to perform His divine duties with full consciousness and deliberate intent. His representation of the Creator Energy is partial for a time and becomes a complete embodiment at one point in His incarnation. At such time, His physical body becomes the vehicle for the actual embodiment and manifestation of the Divine Father on Earth. Master Jesus was such a being – the reason for which He was called "the Christ."
4. The Divine Son appears as a human infant with or without the experience of natural birth. He needs to recollect at first only enough information to allow Him to perform His divine duties with full consciousness and deliberate intent. His representation of the Creator Energy is partial for a time and may become a complete embodiment at one point in the earthly incarnation. At such time, His physical body becomes the vehicle for the actual carrying or temporary embodiment and manifestation of the Divine Mother on Earth. While the Divine Mother is never required to appear in human form, this unique and unprecedented arrangement occurs through the carrying or embodiment of the Divine Father with the intent of reflecting, carrying or temporarily embodying the inherent principles of the Divine Mother. The exceptional task of being present in a humanly-incarnated capacity has been mandated by the current human shift of 2012 so that the Divine Mother can benefit humankind with Her tremendous presence and energy.

---

39 Energy of the Divine Creator (Divine Father and Divine Mother) of the Local Universe, similar to the concept of "Christ Consciousness."

AWAKENING THE NEW CIRCUITS ...

The beings involved in the Divine Plan of 2012 are thus the Divine Sons and Masters who are reflecting, carrying and potentially embodying the different aspects and principles of Source in one capacity or another. They emerge simultaneously for a time and continue manifesting progressively between the years 2004 and 2020. After 2020, their presence and energy is sustained for another 200 to 300 years, which is the time required for Earth and its inhabitants to uphold such a level of advanced consciousness on their own. Each of the beings involved in the Divine Plan is either in human form or in other material or spirit form present on the Earth or within the Milky Way. Depending on the type of being they are and the amount of energy they can withstand, each has a required or *pre-determined circuit* they are linked to. Combined, all circuits intertwine and form a spectacular structure joined at the area of the Central Suns (the core of the galaxy), at the center of your Local Universe and ultimately at the Central Universe, forming a spectacular hexagon-like formation. **See figure 19 on page 85.**

On the other hand, the beings incarnated as humans form a tetrahedron-like shaped structure around the surface of the Earth and are linked through entwining circuits that merge collectively at the earth grid. This massive tetrahedral formation fits within the larger hexagonal shape of the Divine Plan's divine circuits and is thus what connects the earth grid to the core of the universe. These circuits and grids are *the Physical Energy of Source* that is being restored to its original patterning and alignment with Source. Once these grids are re-assembled and complete, Mind and Spirit Energies begin to circulate abundantly within all areas being shifted and the cosmic light and energy of Source begins to pour in.

Since Physical Energy is the energy of the Divine Son, the emerging circuitry becomes thus *alive* through the very beings who embody each aspect of it and *through the process of their individual awakening.* Depending on the type of being they are and the amount of frequency range they are able to sustain, the beings involved in the Divine Plan gradually awaken to their true essence and remember their task by the time it is to be fulfilled – 2012. Each time they re-

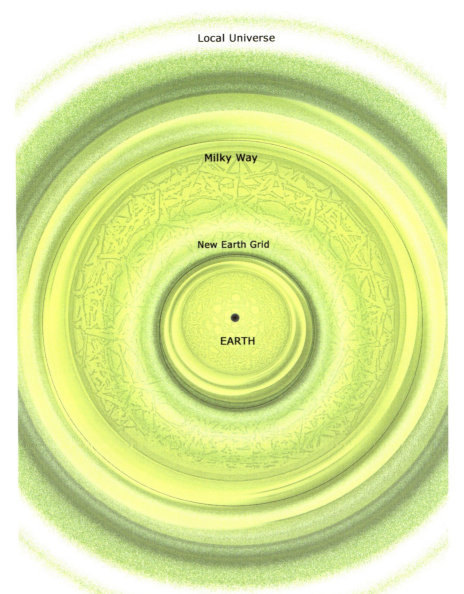

Figure 19: Complete hexagonal circuits of the manifested Divine Plan

member one aspect of this Divine Plan, a portion of the massive divine circuit they carry is ignited and activated. This portion of the new divine grid that is being ignited is the very circuit integrated within their being. Not all beings are required to reach the same amount of remembrance or achieve this remembrance in the same way. They all are required, however, to recollect enough information regarding their predestined circuit and pre-natal contract in order to proceed on their human journey in a conscious and deliberate manner.

THE BEINGS INVOLVED IN THE DIVINE PLAN ...

THE DIVINE FATHER is your direct and original Creator and, through this Divine Plan, has chosen once again to manifest in material form through the presence of the Divine Son. The Divine Father has often materialized in a multitude of ways, through many beings and in varying degrees on the earth plane. Some of your most recognized Masters and Prophets have contributed to His appearance in most memorable and magnificent ways. Through the consecutive presence of the Divine Son, the Divine Father has never actually left the earth plane and has been walking amongst you, through the de-particularized aspects of His being, for the past 2,000 years. However, at the appropriate time, He will manifest once more in the body of a human as a new and original incarnation. Through this new physical embodiment, He brings all aspects and principles of His being – omnipotence, omnipresence, omniscience, Love, Truth, Beauty and Goodness – to the human realm. He has come forth and has chosen to emerge in a most unique and unprecedented arrangement, and, while He does not reveal Himself purposely, He is and can be experienced through telepathic contact and extra sensory perception at will. *This experience, however, is a gradual process* as the human consciousness is unable to grasp completely the tremendous power and energy of this extraordinary being. However, as you awaken on your journey, the energy of the Divine Father becomes increasingly detectable by you.

Due to His massive consciousness, the Divine Father appears in several entities and different locales at once in the being of the Divine Son. He embodies the energy of all the recognized Divine and Ascended Masters of your past history combined and thus may appear as a Divine Master Himself. His energy is thereby dispersed and reassembled once He emerges in physical form. The expanse of His tremendous power allows Him to experience all layers of universal reality at once and thereby affect, uplift and restore all that with which He comes in contact. As a Creator, He is also capable of transforming life forms as He experiences them, simply through the projection of His thought. He works intimately with other Divine Sons and Masters who are also responsible for the actualization of this Divine Plan. He is the creator, director and main power source for all those involved in this magnificent plan.

The Divine Father-Son incarnated in human form will become recognized more fully after 2013 while His human configuration will be, in fact, sustained consecutively by 3 individual beings between 2013 and 2250. When in human form, the Divine Father-Son remains linked to the core of this Local Universe as well as the Central Universe at all times, thereby bringing the energy, frequency range and alignment of your Earth and galaxy into coherent harmony with those of the Central Universe. *The Central Universe, the core of this Local Universe and the Milky Way constitute the Divine Father-Son's circuit.* As He awakens to this Plan, He activates these very areas within the consciousness of humanity, simply by anchoring His light and frequency range within the Earth's structure in a deliberate manner. This process gradually triggers the Earth's physiological, electromagnetic and spiritual shifts and instills the planet's final settling into a new position within the cosmos. **See figure 20 on page 88.**

THE DIVINE SONS, who are still in spirit form, work closely with the incarnated Divine Sons and Masters of similar heritage. These magnificent Creator Beings are capable of withstanding the energy and frequency range of Source – the core of the Local Universe and that of the Central Universe – no matter where they choose to appear and what form they choose to take. There are 3 Divine Sons of the highest Creator Order involved in the Divine Plan on Earth, each

88   The Divine Plan: Beyond 2012

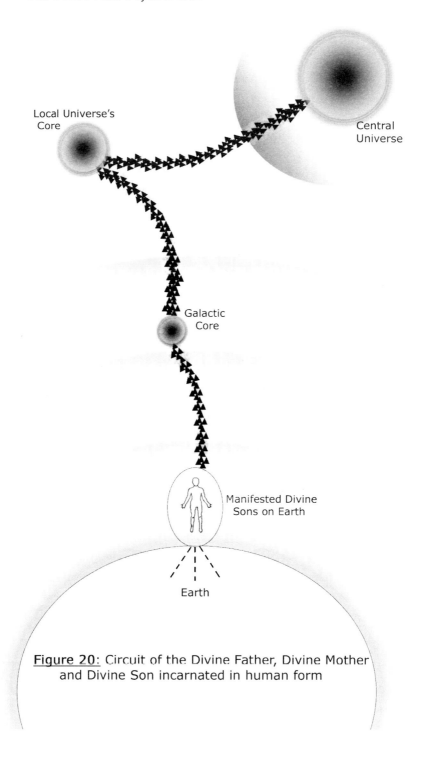

Figure 20: Circuit of the Divine Father, Divine Mother and Divine Son incarnated in human form

representing one or more principles of the Divine Son of Source. While they are in human form, they can be experienced as the same or as separate entities depending on one's ability to discern subtle energy clearly.

The 3 incarnated Divine Sons operate in unison, even if they are physically dispersed throughout the Earth for a time. Each represents a specific principle of the Divine Father and holds a somewhat identical frequency range of the same original being. When on Earth, they display these respective aspects through their individual awakening. Finally, at the appropriate time, they will form a cohesive body on the earth plane that will be recognized as one. The amount of frequency they each are able to carry varies according to their awakening process, but it will eventually manifest an energetic structure on Earth that is trigonometrically coherent with the Mind Energy of the Divine Father of Source. This purposeful delineation in aspects, principles, tasks and awakening allows the emergence of this tremendous unified field in a well-orchestrated and synchronized manner that must manifest perfectly according to other elements and requirements of the Divine Plan on Earth. *The Divine Sons' circuits bypass the earth's grid and connect the entire planetary system with the galactic core, the core of the Local Universe and, in turn, the Central Universe.* **Refer to figure 20 on page 88.**

THE DIVINE MOTHER is your original and direct co-Creator and is the Divine Creator's principles of Love, Truth, Beauty and Goodness. Together with the Divine Father, she co-creates the parameters – time and space – within which this Divine Plan is to unfold. The Divine Mother – not to be confused with feminine energy[40] – is present in physical form through a unique arrangement and distributes Her energy through those beings who are actively involved in this tremendous task. Her essence can be felt as loving energy that infiltrates all aspects of human life. The Divine Mother's energy also sustains the energy of Truth within your system and challenges those structures that are based on falseness and deceit. As you observe human scandals surfacing on your Earth, know that it is the work and energy of your magnificent Divine Mother that are triggering these events. Many beings currently on Earth reflect or carry the energy of the Divine Mother in varied degrees and are now awakening to such

---

40   Feminine aspects or attributes that can be embodied by both male and female material beings.

truth. They are the principle instigators of Love and Truth on Earth and may appear as simple humans with average lives or those in positions of power who are integrated within your political and other governmental and societal structures. While their full remembrance of this Divine Plan and particular involvement occurs gradually, these incarnated beings are nonetheless capable of holding the Divine Mother's tremendous frequency range while in human form, thereby uplifting the areas of human life they encounter on their natural physical journey.

The Divine Mother is carried by 1 primary body in human form but is reflected, carried and represented by 3 other main beings with somewhat similar capabilities. Since the Divine Mother does not technically incarnate in human form, She is carried and reflected by this 1 main body in a most unique and unprecedented arrangement. This unique Divine Master is in fact of the Divine Son lineage and has volunteered to reflect and represent all of the Divine Mother's principles – Love, Truth, Beauty, and Goodness – in a powerful and exquisite manner on the Earth. As the other Masters who also share one or more of these magnificent principles awaken to their true essence, the Divine Mother circuit becomes activated and sustained from 2013 through 2250, which will allow a direct and permanent link to *the core of the Local Universe*, thereby supporting and enhancing the circuits created by the incarnated Divine Father and Divine Sons. **Refer to figures 20 and 21 on pages 88 and 91.**

THE DIVINE ASSEMBLY is the prime group of beings orchestrating this Divine Plan on Earth. This Assembly is comprised of a core group of 12 beings of the highest Divine Order who act as a "supreme court," so to speak, and hold accountable all those who have deliberately harmed your planet and misled your species. The Divine Assembly's members function under the supervision of the Divine Father and the Divine Son and are the keepers of universal agreements. They formulate countless programs, contracts and plans throughout the universes to maintain structure and harmony within the worlds. They are also the instigators of your planet's awakening process and ultimately the reminders of your individual pre-natal contracts.

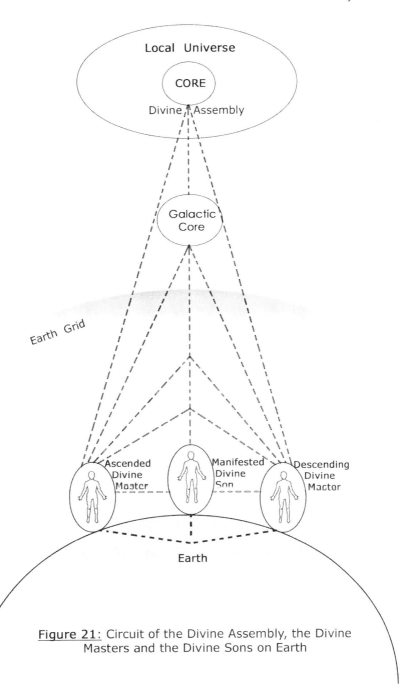

Figure 21: Circuit of the Divine Assembly, the Divine Masters and the Divine Sons on Earth

The Assembly functions on the basis of the Divine Creators' principles of Love, Truth, Beauty and Goodness. Therefore, its work is the result of such understanding and is always permeated with such energy. While there exists an assembly for each universe, galaxy and planetary system, it is the Assembly of the Central Universe that is in charge of planning and carrying out the Divine Plan on Earth. This Assembly remains in continuous contact with the incarnate Divine Sons and Masters throughout their earthly career. While the members of the Divine Assembly do not appear in human form, their work in structure, order, management, peace and harmony permeates through those incarnated Masters on Earth. *The Assembly's circuit involves the systems between the Divine Sons and the Divine Masters on Earth and the core of the Local Universe.* **See figure 21 on page 91.**

The DIVINE MASTERS in human form work in conjunction with the 3 Divine Sons and all other beings involved in the Plan. These Divine Masters are part of the energy field called the Creator Energy, which is the energy of the Divine Father and the Divine Mother at once. These Masters include highly evolved beings of the Teacher Order such as the Melchizedeks who have been continuously working with humans since the beginning of time. There are 7 Master Teachers of the Melchizedek as well as other Universal Teacher and Messenger Orders present in human form, while many of these same orders continue to work and function amongst you in spirit form. Those in human form are awakening and upholding the new light grids being created, while those in spirit form are contributing to their efforts by implanting these tremendous circuits onto the earth plane.

The Universal Master Teachers and Messengers are summoned by the Divine Father of the Central Universe in conjunction with the Divine Father of the Local Universe to voluntarily partake in the tremendous transition of Earth and the Milky Way. They support the Divine Father in His manifestation through the Divine Sons and contribute to this great task of anchoring the Divine Father / Son's pillars of light in various areas of the globe. While some Divine Masters in human form are already aware of the others, not all are currently working together in a conscious and deliberate manner. These Masters are simply recognizing their counterparts – the other Teacher-Masters – as such and allowing the work to unfold through the natural course of human life. This is partially the cause of their apparent disconnection even though they are, in fact, one and the same energy – the Creator Energy. They, in time, all become cognizant and fully aware of their perpetual interconnection and their mutual link to this Divine Plan. Together, *these Masters uphold the circuits between the core of the Milky Way – the area of the Central Suns – and the various galactic cores within the Local Universe*, creating once more a stupendous circuit of great power. **Refer to figure 21 on page 91.**

THE POWER CONTROLLERS are tremendous creatures who maneuver, shift, transform and move energy from one point of the universe to another and transmute energy from one form into another. They comprise various categories and types of beings, including the *Energy Controllers* who are in charge of sustaining the power structure of an entire universe and, also, reflecting the energies blasting from various points within the universe at once. They work in conjunction with the LIFE ARCHITECTS who are in charge of instilling the blueprint within the emerging species. There are 11 beings of the Power Controller and Life Architect Orders who are presently incarnated and/or reflected in human form, while many others remain in spirit form and work simultaneously with the Divine Sons and Masters and those responsible for the main aspects of the Divine Plan. The observable results of their action and involvement appear in all aspects of life on Earth, from atmospheric changes, Earth's pulse and polar shifts to the emergence of the new species.

The Power Controllers are the actual entities upholding and reflecting the various circuits and grids within the universes, galaxies, stars and your planetary system. *Those in human form are responsible for distributing diverse energy and reflecting it properly and precisely from various parts of the Earth, through the galactic core and straight into the universal center.* **Refer to figure 21 on page 91.**

These circuits are of tremendous power and very few beings are capable of upholding or reflecting such massive electricity and electromagnetic charge in human form. While the incarnated humans awaken on their journey and consciously ask to uplift the human condition, it is these Universal Beings who actualize their requests. It is a universal law that all created beings of any order must *ask* in order for these powerful beings to materialize and actualize such demands.

The Life Architects, on the other hand, collaborate fully with the Master Power Controllers and enhance their work, but their task is not to uphold the actual circuit. Rather, they are here to instill the new DNA formulas and activate its frequency range onto the earth plane. They remain connected, however, to their original *circuit linking them directly to the center of this universe*, thus enhancing the circuits of others of the same arrangement.

THE GRAVITY CONTROLLERS are those beings who originate at the Local Universe. They represent and reflect the energy of the original Divine Son as He is the Gravity Controller of the entire universe. These divine beings along with other magnificent PLANETARY AIDS form a group of 13 incarnated beings in human form. While holding similar vibration, they function independently of each other throughout the globe. Their purpose is to continuously maintain the gravitational forces within humanity's consciousness as the major shifts occur and the Earth transitions into a new orbit in space. These powerful beings must sustain the energetic frequency range of hundreds of thousands of humans at a time, a task of tremendous importance and sophistication. *Their circuits are aligned directly with the energy of the Divine Son at the Local Universe and balance continuously your entire system with the Divine Son's gravity pull.* **Refer to figure 21 on page 91.**

GALACTIC LIGHT BEINGS on Earth are those who originate from different areas of the Milky Way, other neighboring galaxies and the Local Universe. 17 such Galactic Light Beings have chosen to incarnate in human form for the purpose of assisting the Divine Sons and Masters in their endeavor to restore harmony and balance to the earth plane. While they appear as normal humans, their electrical wiring is of a non-human nature. This wiring allows them to naturally sustain higher frequencies while in physical form and link to a circuit of tremendous reach. *The Light Beings' circuits are many, but they are primarily connected to the main constellations within your galaxy, the area of the Central Suns and in turn the core of the universe.* The main constellations attached to the Light Beings' circuit are Orion, Pegasus, Lyra, Andromeda and Taurus. **See figure 22 on page 96.** Therefore, their collective circuit is of staggering reach and power. Their sensitive nature enhances their speedy awakening to their true essence and to this Divine Plan.

There are also other GALACTIC BEINGS who are in charge of supporting and enhancing the Divine Plan. These form a confederation dedicated to eradicating disruptive energy within the galaxy. They work under the guidance of the Divine Sons and Masters to harmoniously produce the new structure according to this Plan. These beings are stationed within your galaxy but are not incarnated in human form. They do, however, maintain the links between the different star systems and the Star Beings incarnated on Earth now. Even though intergalactic communications regarding this divine agreement are equally and simultaneously broadcasted at once throughout the Milky Way, the headquarter or hub of this confederation is presently located in Sirius B, which is a satellite office, so to speak, for the main structure within the Pleiades.

STAR BEINGS on Earth are those who originate from different star systems, typically within this galaxy. Similar to the Light Beings, they appear as normal humans while carrying a specific electrical wiring that links them directly to their star or constellation of origin. 33 main Star Beings are currently on Earth and are awakening mostly through the help of their counterparts in their respective original home, who enable them to retrace their true essence and awaken to their truthful destiny on Earth. *The Star Beings' circuit includes Sirius, Arcturus, Polaris, Bellatrix, Centaurus and the Pleiades* among other many stars and constellations that are participating in the current awakening of the star children on Earth. **Refer to figure 22 on page 96.**

Through this process, the incarnated Star Beings are able to uphold the circuits and appropriate frequency range linking them to their respective stars. The Star Beings also carry the formula and DNA of the future human species that will manifest and proliferate on Earth over the next 300 years.

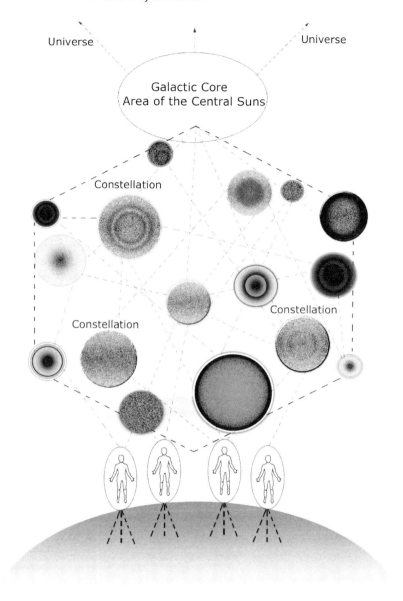

Figure 22: Circuits of the Galactic Light Beings incarnated on Earth

CELESTIAL BEINGS refer to a type of created beings who are of the Seraphic Order. While these beings typically do not incarnate, 12 such creatures are manifested in human form for the purpose of representing or reflecting this loving and compassionate order. They primarily offer protection and guidance for others of the same kind or those partaking in their journey. Their angelic-like appearance and energy exerts tremendous love and empathy. These immaculate beings work with their counterparts of the Seraphic Order who accompany the Divine Sons and Masters in the flesh. While they may not know all of the intricate details of the actual plan, they are certainly cognizant of their individual implication within it. *These loving beings allow the upholding of the planetary system's circuits, which connect the earth grid to the grids of the surrounding planets and in turn with Mars, which is considered the hub of the inner planets of your solar system.* **See figure 23 on page 98.**

MATERIAL BEINGS are those who are originally from this planet and other neighboring evolutionary ones. Their work involves creating and expanding reality on the earth plane or other material worlds. The humans involved in the Divine Plan have evolved farthest and reached levels of enlightenment in their current or other earthly incarnations. Their awakening is gradual but most are able to carry out their mission with partial remembrance as they become powerfully connected to the Creator Energy and the Divine Plan. They hold the highest vibrations among humans, and while they draw their energy from the Sun, *they are linked to the planetary system through energetic circuits. Mars is, in fact, the main focal or juncture point for such circuits.* These humans constitute the highest order of physical beings on Earth and are capable of carrying out tremendous tasks alongside the Masters of the Creator and Teachers Orders.

Other material beings who have originated from other planets, such as Mars, Saturn or Jupiter, appear in human form on Earth, and, similar to other incarnated beings of other systems, they collaborate in creating an intricate energetic circuit that upholds the highest frequencies among physical beings on Earth and within the entire planetary system. While they share similar characteristics as Earth beings in the area of physical makeup, they contribute a great deal

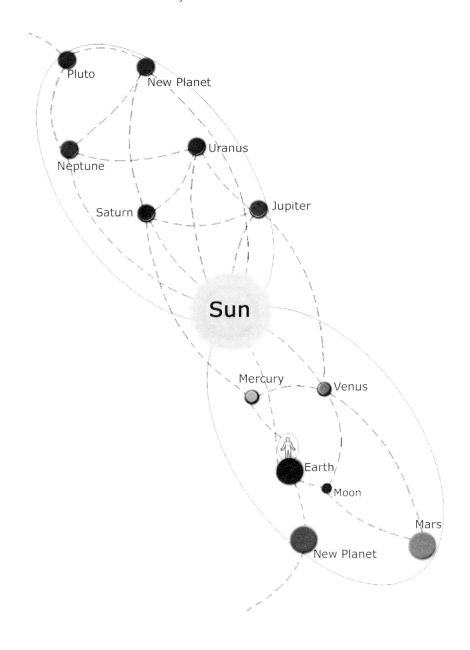

Figure 23: Circuits of the Celestial Beings and other material beings on Earth

to humans in the way of processing information and dealing with their mental and emotional body. They too, however, must gradually awaken to their role in this divine mission and understand the areas in which they contribute to their own spiritual and mind-al growth as well as that of others'. There are 1,000 such material beings, human and otherwise, incarnated on the Earth, upholding planetary circuits and powerfully contributing to the implementation of the Divine Plan. **Refer to figure 23 on page 98.**

Together, there are 1,100 individual beings of various orders in human form who, through the process of awakening to their own essence, are igniting the very circuits they are made of and associated with – thereby manifesting a powerful and massive energetic grid on the Earth and beyond. **See figure 24 on page 102 and figure 19 on page 85.**

It is important to note, however, that all 1,100 are the manifestation of the Divine Father on the Earth in one form or another and, in that respect, can also be referred to as the Divine Son. On the other hand, the 7 aspects of the Divine Father, while carried or represented fully through one individual being each, are also shared by others. Furthermore, the Divine Mother, who is technically a Divine Son is also one of the 7 aspects of the original Divine Father formula. This means, that no being among the above-described 1,100 is totally separate or uniquely configured outside the entire Divine Father-Son structure that comprises all 1,100 aspects at once.

6

The Second Coming

The Second Coming is the completion of an earth cycle that had been misaligned or inconsistent with the original cosmic blueprint and divine principles. It is the process by which the time / space continuum can no longer exist within this false configuration and begins to spin into a new cycle called the *Rejuvenation Phase,* regenerating itself through an extensive and complex system. The Second Coming is thus the beginning of Earth's new cycle on a geophysical level, but also corresponds to the emergence of those beings who have instigated this very event. These are the Divine Sons and Earth Teachers who are capable of carrying the highest frequencies possible within a human body and ushering humanity into this new age through teaching, healing and other tremendous energetic tasks.

Such advent, prophesied repeatedly by many but not yet actualized, coincides with the awakening of 1,100 particles of the divine principles that were first implanted 2,000 years ago through the manifestation of the Divine Father in physical form. While the Divine Father has been embodied on Earth in varied ways by many Divine Masters throughout the history of the Earth, it is the energy carried last by the Divine Master Jesus that remained amongst you since that time and is now resurfacing in the bodies of your contemporary Divine Sons and Masters.

The actual energy of the Divine Father that the Master Jesus carried during His human incarnation was dislodged from His being prior to His departure from Earth and remained implanted on the earth plane in the body of 13 beings at first and 110 beings subsequent to

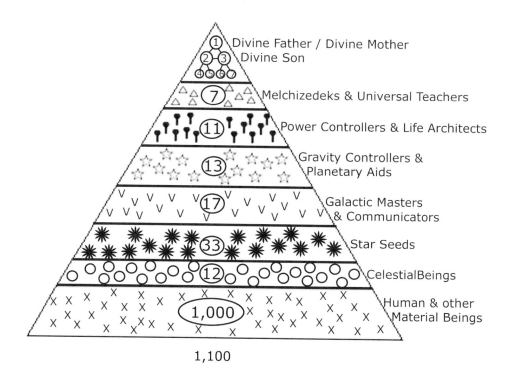

Figure 24: Distribution of the 1,100 particles of the Divine Son in human form between 2012 and 2250

His departure. These 110 beings have replicated themselves through a re-generation process – or reincarnation – to produce 1,100 particles 2,000 years later. While the Divine Father energy was received by everyone on the earth plane, it was *recognized, acknowledged and carried* by those 110 individuals who went about proclaiming the work of this Divine Master and His teachings in the subsequent years. The continual incarnations of these original 110 beings has now produced 1,100 particles of the same original Divine Father energy. The Second Coming marks the completion of this collective incarnation cycle and the full awakening of all 1,100 particles of the Divine Father energy. This awakening and emergence *is* the Second Coming as the very awakening process activates the divine particles within the consciousness of those embodying them and brings these principles forth to the conscious material planes. When this awakening occurs, the acceleration of the global human potential increases a minimum of one thousand-fold and thrusts Earth's consciousness into a new dimensional reality all together.

While it is not necessary for all 1,100 beings to awaken fully in each incarnation, through the Second Coming all particles do awaken to the highest degrees possible in order to implement their tremendous tasks. Those embodying the highest proportions or larger aspects of the Divine Father initiate the collective awakening and lead Earth's entire reality into the next era. These teachers and leaders include 3 beings utilizing the same vehicle – or physical body – for 300 years jointly. They have chosen this configuration and process in order to sustain the highest form of Divine Father energy on the Earth until the planet is able to settle into the New Era of Love and Light and create a new momentum of self-sustenance, self-maintenance and self-regeneration. This being in human form, who is a 7-aspect Divine Son, embodies the second aspect of the First Trinity or Creator-Source – the Universal Son – and the first aspect of the Divine Creator of your Local Universe – the Divine Father / Son. This Divine Son's consciousness encompasses multi-universal reality and relays the Universal Son / Divine Father energy from Source into the universe He is assigned to.

This 7-aspect Divine Son is also de-particularized in 7 aspects – or separate entities within the human consciousness – and performs astounding duties that include maneuvering the electromagnetic fields of the Earth according to the Divine Plan; initiating Earth's polar shift at the propitious time; reflecting powerful divine energies throughout the globe during meditations and prayers; opening the Mind Energy, Spirit Energy and Physical Energy channels between the Earth and Source; awakening, communicating and informing other incarnated Sons and Masters of the imminent changes and their respective roles; reflecting light and sound energies back into the solar system and beyond; merging with humanity's consciousness and reflecting massive light that triggers global spiritual awakenings, healings and shifts; collaborating telepathically with state officials on implementing the relevant changes to bring about the Divine Plan; aligning the human and the earth consciousness with the universal grids and Source; and, more importantly, intervening in the face of serious crisis such as in the case of nuclear propulsion or perilous excesses of nuclear waste. The reign of this Divine Son is 200 to 300 years, which is shared by 2 associate Sons who emerge at the propitious times. This means that within the next 300 years, three beings of the same order utilize the same or a similar body consecutively in order to remain in human form and within the human consciousness.

Within the same time frame, the Divine Mother emerges in the reflection of 1 principal being in human form. This being represents the Divine Mother's principles collectively in a most unique arrangement and agreement. The Divine Mother in human form is supported by 3 main individual bodies as well as many others reflecting and representing Her principles in varied degrees and in diverse forms.

Simultaneously, other Divine Masters of the highest order also emerge in human form to display complementary teachings and tasks. Among those are 7 beings who are currently – or will be – reflecting similar properties as those of the 7-aspect Divine Son in different proportions and at different intervals and thus reflecting somewhat similar deity representations. These Divine Sons include the Universal Teachers, who display and reflect the aspects of the Divine Father and Mother of your Local Universe. Following these brilliant teachers are 11 divine beings of the Power Controller, Energy Reflector and Life Architect Orders, reflecting the aspects of the Divine Father and Mother. These beings are responsible for the proper implanting of the new species and the reflective energies between the planet and its cosmic neighbors. Simultaneously, 13 Planetary Aids and Gravity Controllers, representing the 2 aspects of the Divine Son and Divine Mother, also emerge. They are responsible for Earth's electromagnetic pulse and gravity shifts. Following this category are 17 Galactic Beings and Masters responsible for reestablishing intergalactic communication and spirit reflectivity within the Milky Way and beyond. They represent 1 or 2 deity aspects of the Local Universe. Following are 33 highly evolved Star Seeds who are carrying the new genetic encoding of the future Earth species. They are responsible for the proper promulgation of this new encoding within the earth plane. Following the Star Seeds are 12 Celestial Beings of the Seraphic Order who help instill tremendous love and compassion globally. Finally, 1,000 material beings of the highest order from the earth plane and beyond also simultaneously emerge. Their awakening is instrumental in lifting the mass consciousness of humanity that has been trapped in wrongdoing for prolonged times and in implementing the concept of divinity within the earth plane. The awakening of all 1,100 individual entities to this grand plan is sufficient to fuel the physical manifestation of the 5th deity of the Local Universe on Earth – the energy of the Divine Father / Mother – as well as charge the entire humanity with the same divine blueprint. The completion of the collective awakening is expected to be fulfilled by the end of the year 2012.

It is important to note that the group of 1,100 Divine Beings in human form is *not a hierarchy* in the sense of importance or power. While each indeed carries a different amount or mass of the same Creator Energy, all 1,100 particles fit in one cohesive structure holding a *unified vibration* that allows and triggers the shifts on your planet. Therefore, the tasks of each individual entity are equal to its consciousness mass while simultaneously contributing to the entire collective structure. In this context, each being is neither more important nor more powerful, but rather each individual is holding a unique amount and aspect of the Creator Energy consciousness in a precise formula that implements the overall physical manifestation of the Divine Plan.

In addition to the 1,100 Divine Beings appearing in human form, there exist entire spectrums of invisible Universal Beings from various orders who remain in spirit form. These beings include Archangels, Celestial Beings of the Seraphic Order and countless Universal Messengers, Guides and Aids, assisting in the translation of information, communication between the worlds and with the incarnated individuals' guidance system. The intricate participation of all these visible and invisible magnificent beings is what allows the impeccable and seamless manifestation of the Divine Plan. However, while it is these 1,100 individual beings who are able to *instigate* single-handedly their tremendous tasks, the Divine Plan involves *all humanity* and is inclusive of all beings of the Earth and beyond.

7

Birthing A New Species

Your species occupies a string of energy farthest from the Source and thus the infinitesimal consciousness of your evolutionary life requires millennia of mind expansion in order to perfectly grasp the meaning of the Creator-Source and the mysteries of Creation. However, regardless of your remoteness, each individual created being carries an *equal* amount of the Divine Creator – Divine Father and Divine Mother – that is relative to its consciousness mass and that remains encoded within its very essence. Therefore, all beings hold an inherent divine blueprint but may need a different time span, so to speak, to achieve such a perfected understanding. That is why you are continuously assisted with your expansion by spirit beings who are experienced in such admirable tasks, until humanity reaches permanent and advanced levels of enlightenment.

The creation of a new species on Earth consists of implanting new genetic encodings that allow evolutionary beings to process mind and spiritual expansion with greater speed and reach the higher realms of divinity with more clarity and precision. The emergence of such a species coincides with many factors that include the awakening of the Divine Sons and Masters on Earth, the appearance of the *First Temple,* the shifts in the Earth's genetic encodings and the geophysical changes affecting the earth plane as well as its neighboring worlds.

APPEARANCE OF THE FIRST TEMPLE ...

As each being involved in the Divine Plan gradually awakens to his/her true identity, a magnificent structure begins to appear within the earth plane, creating new energy forms and formulas that ignite the dormant divine lineage in every human soul. This structure is in the form of a temple that combines properties of both material and spiritual origins in such a way as to merge both realities together. At the appearance of this semi-material temple, most humans begin to sense and experience the emergence of the New Era. New light formations and energy patterns appear in the skies everywhere while originating in the First Temple. It is also in this First Temple that spirit beings of the highest order – the Divine Sons, Masters and Teachers – can appear in plain view and interact freely with the material beings on the planet. This first semi-material structure, which possesses over 250,000 "seating" capacity, is first constructed at the galactic headquarters and is transported to an approximate location within the current line of the Arctic Circle of the Earth. Subsequent to the implanting of this magnificent structure, other such edifices begin to appear throughout the globe as *satellite temples*, so to speak, linking up at once approximately 3,300,000 beings across the entire planet to the main area of the First Temple.

The arrival of the First Temple onto the earth plane coincides with the polar shift, marking the beginning of the New Era and the emergence of a new species. This temple acts as a fueling station and funnel between the worlds, allowing a new form of energy to become implanted permanently onto the earth plane at strategic positions within the new hexagonal grid. The implanting of such energy alters the Earth's electromagnetic frequency range, allowing the new species to be born and sustained for the millennia to come. The arrival of the new species also corresponds with the Divine Sons' awakening on the earth plane as they are, themselves, the carriers of the genetic encodings of the temple and the new species all at once.

THE NEW GENETIC ENCODINGS ...

The appearance of the First Temple implies the implantation of the energy that supports new life on Earth. This implantation triggers a spontaneous fueling, so to speak, that ignites the Earth's atmosphere and replaces its old electromagnetic energy with new frequencies and vibrations. Such an event produces spectacular electrical light showers and displays throughout the atmosphere, resembling the aurora phenomenon, and triggers the atmosphere to become highly powered with electric currents and light waves. These tremendous power surges, initiated by sudden and intermittent solar calibrations and movements, may interfere with and break down the current power structures for a time. However, the new emerging electrical atmosphere becomes anchored within the earth plane in its stead and is eventually harnessed to produce continuous energy that fuels the entire globe while supporting the organic DNA of the new species.

Along with the tremendous atmospheric shifts, your new genetic encodings begin to occur as a result of a mutation of the current codes that preserve the human characteristics, namely in relation to the way you assimilate information as well as absorb light. This new encoding is achieved mathematically by a sequence of infinite numbers, determining how each individual begins to spontaneously and perfectly match the vibration of the divine form. This means that every hydrogen-bonded atom in your physical body becomes activated through a new DNA with a mathematical sequence – 666.12 1212.181818.242424.303030.363636... – that spontaneously aligns each cell with the new encoded atoms of your atmosphere, your planet and, in turn, the Milky Way. This atomic alignment automatically opens the energetic channels within your physical body in such a way as to absorb more cosmic light and the new form of energy now present on the Earth.

DIVINE DNA AND HUMAN DNA ...

The *divine DNA* relates to the Mind, Spirit and Physical Energy aspects of your new being that co-exist with your *genetic DNA*, which relates to the humanly-inherited aspect of your being. As such, the 3 distinct bodies[41] – the mind, spirit and physical self – become interrelated into one cohesive form alongside the humanly-inherited DNA, in such a way as to allow a spontaneous multi-dimensional and clearly defined experience of reality. The new vibrations or frequencies of the 3 bodies are derived from a divine formula separate from the human DNA and therefore display different electrical waves and patterns within the physical brain waves. However, when aligned in such a coherent manner, as in the case of your new species, the vibrations or frequencies of the mind, spirit and physical bodies as well as those of the human self become interrelated in a form that only a new type of *Light Being* can uphold. This species – the new form of Light Being – is currently being born on the earth plane. The new species is one that has perfectly merged its divine and human DNA's, allowing instant and clear recognition of the self from its inception as pure consciousness to its current physical manifestation.

The divine DNA involved in the creation of the new species is characterized by a formula that includes billions of light particles from varied locations within the universal structure. Each formula is unique to the individual and represents its *lineage*. For example, when a being originates from a star system 1,000 light years away, her divine DNA includes those particles of light in the Spirit Self aspect of her being even as she appears in human form. If this same being, while originating 1,000 light years away, has also integrated, at some point in her history, the structure of other planetary systems 500, 300, 100 and 50 light years away, for example, her divine DNA now carries light particles from those respective systems as well. *The amount* as well as *the type* of light particles integrated in the Spirit Self of each being thus determine the origin and lineage of this being. Once in human form, it is through the Spirit Self – the Spirit Energy portion of the self – that each being is able to retrace its own history, divine patterns and heritage, as well as its reasons for earthly incarnation among other things. **See figure 7 on page 23.**

---

41 Not to be confused with the astral, mental and soul body of the human energy field. See figure 7 on page 23 for more details.

DIVINE DNA AND THE MASCULINE AND FEMININE ASPECTS ...

The divine DNA of each evolutionary being is derived from and originally conceived at the Source, which is the center of your Local Universe, by your divine parent the Divine Creator – the Divine Father and the Divine Mother. The divine DNA therefore carries the characteristics of both in an infinite number of formulas based on the 7 aspects of the Divine Creator. While the term "Father" is being used to describe an infinite being such as your Creator, this term does not refer to your understanding of human father or relate to your concept of masculinity. Here, the term "Father" is simply a metaphorical term that allows the human mind to connect with the first aspect of divinity through a unique pathway, so to speak. In fact, the human father is an attempt to pave the way for the human mind to attain this distinct experience of the Divine Father. Similarly, the term "Mother" – as in Divine Mother – does not refer to a maternal or feminine aspect. Rather, it is simply another aspect of divinity distinct from – yet conjoint with – the Divine Father.

The Divine Father and Mother are also a form of energy: Mind Energy and Spirit Energy respectively. At Source, there are no feminine and masculine aspects but rather there is a system of polarity that characterizes the movement, direction and rotation of energy. What is referred to as "masculine" can be compared to a linear force in one defined direction whereas "feminine" can be compared to a circular-like or recursive movement. Mind Energy – or Divine Father – is considered to be a masculine aspect whereas Spirit Energy – or Divine Mother – is more elliptical or circular and can be described as feminine. Physical Energy – or Divine Son – on the other hand, contains both masculine and feminine aspects at once in order to sustain the wave oscillation of both Mind and Spirit Energy in physical form.

When translated into a physical reality, such wave oscillations of energy appear as physical characteristics – such as the sex of the human being – as well as attributes and manifest, in human terms, as aggressive or passive, masculine or feminine. However, these attributes do not correlate necessarily with the Divine Father or Divine Mother aspects. Therefore, when incarnating in human form you may appear as a male and carry or reflect mostly the Spirit Energy of the Divine Mother or appear as a female and carry or reflect mostly the Mind Energy of the Divine Father.

PROPERTIES OF THE NEW SPECIES' DNA ...

From a divine geometry perspective, the human genome transmutes into *an all-form structure* fitting all the geometric forms in existence that are based on infinite numbers and sequences from the primal tetrahedral structure to the infinite spherical structure. The new encodings happen simultaneously with the transformation of the earth grid, from a basic dodecahedron shape – that now allows access to 32 dimensions – to a new hexagon-like shape within an indestructible infinite holographic sphere. This sphere contains all infinite shapes in existence and allows access to an infinite number of dimensions. This means that the human body begins to transmute itself into a new form of light body that can appear in many different shapes, as desired, at once. This evolutionary process allows you to communicate with other beings of different form or origin in an elaborate manner and without the use of language simply by matching their shape or, in other words, their vibration. This also implies that you are now able to translate back and forth from human to spirit form at will without interrupting your material incarnation. However, regardless of the shape you take at any given time, your original divine DNA encoding is your infinite identity and leaves no room for error, so to speak, regarding who you really are as an essence or pure consciousness prior to your original materialization. This, in turn, eliminates the need for material identity verification as your new light body becomes who you are – vibrationally and socially. Moreover, this magnificent process allows you to commune directly with all life forms while your light body itself becomes your ultimate vehicle for intergalactic travel and communication.

From an electrical perspective, the information being retrieved by your physical brain begins to utilize 3 distinct mind channels of communication: one leading to the human or planetary circuits, another to the interplanetary and galactic grids and yet another linked to the universal circuitry – all without any interference or obstruction from the human channels. These distinct mind circuits first interact with your physical aspect through the cerebral cortex portion of the brain into the hypothalamus and the pineal gland, which is responsible for absorbing and reflecting light. Information is then distributed throughout your physical body alongside the peripheral nervous system channels by way of minuscule meridians. The main cross-over between the human, galactic and universal mind channels is through the pineal gland. The human or planetary channels, however, while also implanted into the central nervous system via the cerebral cortex, are distributed throughout the physical body by way of the limbic system, the hypothalamus, the endocrine system and the peripheral nervous system. The merging of these 3 mind channels into one coherent system is made possible through stupendous electrical loop wiring and transmission systems at the atomic level, the frequency range of which exceeds the speed of light while giving the illusion of being static and material. There is, however, an astounding system of energy distribution jolting back and forth between these 3 distinct Mind Energy circuits within the infinitesimal formula and intelligence of the human atom. The frequency waves' distinction between the divine and the human mind channels allows information to be transmitted from Source into the galactic center and in turn into your planetary system in a flawless manner, providing the Individual in human form with clear recognition and discernment regarding the origin of the information being downloaded in and out of his/her brain circuits. The electric wiring of the future human brain is thus characterized by the frequency wave's discernment between the human and divine mind channels. This discernment is accompanied by an extraordinary shift in consciousness as each being becomes fully aware of who they really are at the time of physical incarnation and the way in which they can deliberately begin to carry out their evolutionary earthly purpose. Furthermore, the functioning of the new human brain allows it to maintain higher frequencies, *obliterating completely the existence of the subconscious or unconscious mind.*

On a chemical level, the distribution of elements in the human body and individual cells becomes less porous, so to speak, as to allow little or no foreign substances to interfere with the natural metabolic mechanism. The increased amounts of oxygen, hydrogen and helium within the atomic structure of the human body begin to match the atmosphere and the Sun's energy in a coherent manner, retrieving the energy the human body requires for life sustenance directly from the Sun and the solar system atmosphere. Physical illness soon becomes a pattern of the past, while the need for sleep and energy uptake is also reduced dramatically.

The new chemical composition of the human body requires little or an insignificant amount of maintenance, so to speak, as it matches the new highly electric atmosphere and thus becomes perfectly aligned with the source of life at the core of the universe. This shift naturally allows you to focus on new priorities and interests in your physical life, namely the creation of healthy trends that support the newly instilled systems, from meditation and spirituality to cosmic contemplation and expansion. While your brain potential is *gradually* increased to approximately 70% by the end of the century, the nutrition required for such a mechanism to function properly becomes of utmost significance. It is not the amount but the quality and the purer forms of energy that you now require to upkeep your magnificent new apparatus.

This electrical wiring and chemical distribution provide the new species with a drastically new life experience. The clarity and discernment of the mind channels allow not only a spontaneous connectivity with the planet but also easier access to other frequencies and realities. Conscious telepathic communication as well as the perception of subtle energy simply become commonplace. The actual geophysical and atmospheric changes of the planet as well as the reconstruction of Earth's axes through the light anchoring process now allow the new humans to experience life differently. The simultaneous transmutation of the new human's physical brain and genomes are what is needed for such an experience. The planetary shifts as well as the species' DNA are synchronized in such a way as to allow a gradual and natural emergence of the new species beginning in the year 2020 and spanning over a period of 200 to 300 years. Once fully emerged, the new human species interacts with a highly evolved reality and thus continues contributing to human growth and expansion. Global humanistic activities, highly sophisticated education, exquisite arts and expanded cosmic sciences are but a few examples of the interests of this brilliant new species.

This magnificent species is also supported by a newly-formed animal and plant life consciousness, the purpose of which is to monitor the pulse and breathing of the planet. Gradually, coherence of the brain patterns and heart pulse begins to occur between the different species and the earth. This means that the various rhythmic pulses of the human brain and the human heart become perfectly coherent with the pulse and breathing patterns of the new earth, the animal kingdom and the plant and mineral life. This elegant dance and exquisite new experience finally allow a seamless and perpetual merging of the divine realms within your earthly reality.

8

Timing Of The Divine Plan

The Divine Plan begins at the Central Universe where it is initiated and organized by the Divine Father in conjunction mainly with the Divine Son, the Divine Mother, the Divine Assembly and the Divine Masters of the Local Universe. As the Divine Plan is finalized and approved by the Major Universe's courts and legislative bodies, it is dispensed simultaneously throughout the Local Universe into which it is destined to manifest. However, due to the staggering expanse of the universes and the billions of light years between the Central Universe, the core of the Local Universe and the Milky Way, the materialization of such a plan on your Earth appears gradually over a period of time when perceived from a linear or chronological standpoint. For example, as one idea is initiated in one hour in the area of the Central Suns of the Milky Way, which is approximately 26,000 light years away, it takes approximately 3 days for that event to manifest on the earth plane. The further the onset of the idea or plan, the longer manifestation span it requires on the earth plane. As such, the Divine Masters such as Buddha, Jesus, Enoch or Krishna appeared in a chronological manner on your Earth when, in fact, they had been "dispensed" from the core of the Local Universe all at once, as one same energy and for one single purpose. Due to the magnitude of this energy as well as the physical distance between the core of the universe and your Earth, these beings have appeared as separate entities at separate historical moments and in separate locales on your planet. This phenomenon of time delay, so to speak, is also due to the transition from infinite to more finite, from timeless to time and from absolute to limited, from spiritual to material and from one zero point within physical space into another. When viewed from Source, however, where this divine energy was originally conceived, the de-particularization of this energy is still considered *one simultaneous and complete event.*

Similar to these divine entities who "arrived" at different historical moments, the *energy and information* that they carried also began as one simultaneous event dispensed from the Source and broadcasted within your entire universe, galaxy, planets and stars all at once. You on Earth, however, begin to feel the effect of such tremendous energy only when it has all landed, so to speak, bringing the original conception of the event to closure. The time of this final landing appears gradually between the years of 2000 and 2012. However, to restrict such a grand event to one specific time or date as recognized by your human calendar – when the effect of such tremendous energy is suddenly experienced in one instant by everyone all at once and all over your planet – assumes that distance and time is similar between the worlds and space at large. Such is simply not the case. From Earth's perspective, such a phenomenon is *gradual* and requires several crucial components in order for it to be totally and completely experienced and actualized on the Earth. These components include: astronomical alignments and configurations; the emergence of divine entities on Earth; the anchoring of the Creator Energy through light and sound frequencies in specific earthly locations; the collapse of the old systems; the global awakening of consciousness on Earth and the *recognition* of this emerging reality, among many other elements and requirements – all of which cannot be bound to one date and time on your human linear calendar.

The major astronomical alignments involved in the Divine Plan have been many over the past 2,000 years. However, it is the alignment of May 2000 that brought this cycle of planetary configurations necessary to the actualization of the Divine Plan to closure. This planetary alignment is the actual implanting of the Divine Creator frequency – the original blueprint of Source – on the earth plane. However, as suggested above, the *effects* of such implanting are felt sporadically over a period of time, culminating in 2012.

The physical anchoring of the Divine Creator Energy also began on a material level outside the capitol of Egypt in the year 2000, through the participation of divine and human entities at once. This anchoring has re-established the severed main energetic axis that links Earth to the outer worlds. It is at this location that Earth's umbilical cord linking you to the center of the universe resides, and, through this light and sound anchoring, the divine flow and pillars of light from Source have been re-instilled and activated. This was the first global light anchoring of its kind and has many sequels that have yet to be actualized. These light anchoring events take place at specific locations where energetic earth axes have been dismantled or tampered with. The more pronounced impact of such events, however, is only experienced in the years 2012-2013 and beyond.

NEW LEVELS OF CONSCIOUSNESS ...

The awakening of global human consciousness began decades ago, but it is a *new level of awareness* altogether, introduced in the year 2000, that all now attain in order to consciously remember and actively participate in the Divine Plan. New energies that emerge after the year 2000 contain the very vibration of the Divine Creator Energy and become effortlessly recognized by those involved in the Divine Plan.

STAGES OF THE NEW ERA ...

The manifestation of the Divine Plan triggers transformations and reforms on all levels of earthly existence and requires several stages to set the Earth onto a perpetual course of enlightenment. These stages, characterized by increased reality awareness and a full cognition of other worlds, span over a hundred to several hundred years each. Although information, communication and awareness of far-flung cosmic realities are already in existence, these stages allow *the full realization and physical actualization* of these cosmic realities in a gradual and progressive manner.

The emergence of the New Era has technically already begun in the year 2000. Some are already cognizant of the sporadic signs of this age through the increase in political and corporate scandals and the incessant demand for truth. These signs are also felt through the noticeable unusual weather patterns or the magnitude and frequency of devastating storms. This trend of sporadic signs continues on various levels through 2009 when more significant earth changes occur. At this time, the subtle signs become obvious facts that eventually halt the current human existence worldwide. While the new energies are simultaneously felt throughout these earth changes, it is only after 2012, however, that these powerful energies become more apparent and constant. Between 2012 and 2020, the rebuilding of the planet occurs, allowing the emergence of new systems and structures based on Truth and the divine principles of Source. This positive momentum becomes the new base of life for all beings on the Earth, eventually eradicating, in 2020, the remaining but insignificant evil energy from human consciousness altogether.

As of 2020, the New Era of Love and Light begins to take new form, instilling systems, through various stages, that will remain in place for millennia to come. In *the First Stage of the New Era,* which truly begins as early as 2013 but culminates in 2020, humanity at large begins to realize that the first stage of the New Era of Enlightenment is in fact being actualized. This awareness includes planetary consciousness, which means that all humans become aware of their planetary citizenship and begin to implement great projects, supporting the growth and prosperity of the entire planet – rather than focusing on the needs of the individual states. The primary goal of this new society is to remain truthful to its inherent potential for survival as one complete and whole organism. The first stage of the New Era spans approximately 100 years. *The Second Stage of the New Era* widens the awareness of humanity from the planetary to the solar system and is characterized by the full recognition of other civilizations within the solar system. This awareness brings about real communication and physical interaction with beings and intelligences of other-than-human origin. This stage spans approximately over

300 to 500 years. *The Third Stage of the New Era* opens the galactic doorways fully and allows the full physical recognition and realization of galactic intelligences. This stage also spans from 300 to 500 years. *The Fourth Stage* brings full cognition of the Local Universe and spans over 100 years. *The Fifth, Sixth and Seventh stages* continue to widen the full reality of the multi-universal structures and organization, ultimately leading to the full reality and *physical recognition* of the Divine Creator and the Creator-Source.

Together, the stages of the New Era create a timeless bond between the evolutionary worlds and the divine realities of Source and are based on undeniable Truth and exquisite Love. Earth requires several hundred years to achieve all stages required for your planetary evolution, but the events of 2012 mark the true beginning of the glorious era that finally settles your world in Peace, Love and Light for millennia to come.

9
Geophysical Events

    The amount of nuclear and toxic material as well as the active nuclear reactors that are present on your planet at this time create extremely volatile circumstances, hindering the Earth's ability to survive a geophysical event of larger magnitude without serious debilitating consequences. While Earth has endured many massive cataclysms throughout its history, one substantial volcanic eruption today can indeed annihilate this planet and its inhabitants entirely, due to the accidental nuclear and other toxic spills that may ensue. Additionally, some geophysical and cataclysmic events – such as wars, atmospheric warming and manipulation[42] or premeditated attacks of aggression – are also being orchestrated by a few misguided humans and other outer-worldly beings.[43] These beings are present on the Earth for the purpose of instilling a new world order based on total control and fear, in complete isolation from Source. This seems to be a final attempt on the part of these misguided souls to dominate a juvenile species such as your humanity and experiment with its brain capacity and genetic potential. However, such efforts will now be counteracted or neutralized through the Divine Plan unfolding on the Earth. This is precisely the very reason such divine intervention is occurring now – to circumvent Earth's more-than-likely demise in the face of its invisible and seemingly invincible oppressive opponents.

---

42   Global warming due to human-made toxic fumes and deliberate weather pattern manipulation.
43   Material beings of other planetary systems that exist within the earth plane but remain invisible to humans due to the time / space continuum and their vibrational range.

While some geophysical events are being instigated purposely by humans and others, as above mentioned, these events may still be predicted according to the amount of momentum they have already accumulated. Also, while it is difficult to formulate a linear timetable for the manifestation of all other natural geophysical changes – those orchestrated through the Divine Plan – due to the massive *multi-dimensional* aspects involved, it is possible to predict what may actually occur with 98% or more probability within a few moments of the predicted event. The laws of physical manifestation dictate that energy that has accumulated enough momentum, but has acquired a 92% or less probability of occurrence, can still be avoided and may never materialize. Those energies that have acquired 92% to 98% momentum of probability can still be altered or delayed before they manifest physically. However, those energies that accumulate a 98% or greater amount of probability have an inevitable physical manifestation and consequence. Such a general but highly-probable timetable regarding the geophysical changes that occur on the earth plane between 2000 and 2020 is described below. These events occur sporadically at first and gradually increase in frequency, culminating between 2008 and 2011.

GEOMAGNETIC ASPECTS OF THE DIVINE PLAN …

Beginning in the year 2000, increased solar flares instigate the onset of a planetary polar shift, triggering significant geomagnetic changes on the earth plane. While the more obvious physical changes that ensue can be detected as early as 2007, the total manifestation of this event spreads over a period of approximately 20 years, ending in the year 2020. Some of the observed effects include reversals and modifications in the Earth's magnetic field, a recalibration of the Earth's tectonic pulse and changes in the Earth's axis and rotation cycle. These changes indubitably affect the Earth's atmosphere, the eco-system, the plant and mineral life and create a type of dynamic that prompts a great shift in the experience of reality on the Earth.

As of 2007, the polar shift engenders tremendous electromagnetic showers that occur within the earth grid, bombarding the planet with new energy that remains collected within the stratosphere and ionosphere of the planet. The areas most affected by this energetic momentum are North America and the European Peninsula. This movement creates pressure over the American–European tectonic plate, causing it to shift into a diagonal position – first energetically separating these 2 continents and subsequently separating North America from Europe further. By the end of 2007, South America aligns electromagnetically with Europe first and then Africa, isolating North America's position even further. The collective energy of South America and Africa triggers the planet's magnetic field to begin rotating in one direction south of the equator, in the opposite direction of the magnetic field located north of the equator. While these events may not be observable through the naked eye, they can be traceable through electromagnetic measuring equipment available on Earth.

The beginning of 2008 marks the appearance of a new light form, facilitated by the magnetic shifting, through an aperture within the earth grid. This new form of energy and light reaches the northwestern coastal areas of the North American continent first and progressively covers the entire United States in a "diagonal" manner. The new light, accompanied by the appearance of outer space crafts and non-human beings in varied areas, is clearly and undeniably visible by many. This new light, which appears as a "liquid-like" range of reddish tones, gradually fills the earth grid and eventually covers the entire planet. The arrival of this tremendous electromagnetic light triggers a consciousness awakening process on a global scale as several simultaneous governmental outbursts occur around the globe. As government and corporate officials continue to be expelled from their posts in a synchronized manner, the actual shifting of the electromagnetic currents begins to materialize. About November 2008, the proper electromagnetic channels of the earth plane are re-configured and the new energies begin to pour in. At this time, the polar shift, which had begun technically 2 millennia ago, is finally materialized and all energy grids and circuits of the planet, within its parameters and within the galactic structure, are now perfectly instilled. With this new energy now profusely present, subtle energy as well as spirit beings become more and more perceivable, creating a combination of great confusion, chaos and excitement within the masses.

Once the earth grids and energy channels have been re-aligned with the galactic core, the actual *separation of the worlds* begins. 2009 marks the beginning of such global events that bring about the obliteration of the old patterns for the purpose of creating the new. Much is being observed at this stage in the world's history that affects life as you know it, on all levels and in varied ways. The repercussions of such extraordinary events are far-reaching in many observable areas as they destabilize the current organizations and structures of the planet – such as governmental, educational, scientific, socio-economic, religious, etc. – and shatter the currently established ruling class, duly replacing it by another. The new earth magnetic cycles begin to emerge after these global upheavals have subsided – at the dawn of 2013 – and powerfully create a new reality based on the principle of long lasting Love and Light.

THE EARTH'S AXIS AND ASTRONOMICAL CHANGES …

The first observable electromagnetic shift is triggered by the Sun, which as of 2012 begins a new cycle of calibration that enables a new octave of light to reach the Earth. This means that light energy – which contains cosmic information – becomes available in larger quantities, so to speak, allowing a much awaited turn of events. The increase in solar energy and flares facilitates the production of hydrogen and subsequently helium-charged fragments, which in turn stimulates the environment in such a way as to produce more energy going back and forth between Earth and its planetary neighbors. This exchange of cosmic information is nothing but the birth of new systems of light and colors emerging simultaneously in various parts of your world.

The creation or apparition of new light and color energy globally affects the realignment of the Earth within its own solar system and, in turn, within the Milky Way. This realignment occurs through the altering of the planetary axis, which controls or contributes to seasonal changes on your planet. As early as 2007, your Earth's axis begins to shift gradually to approximately 19° from its perpendicular orbital plane, allowing its new trajectory – which facilitates more cosmic light absorption – to implement new temperature control, so to speak, or a re-organized seasonal experience on the Earth. The atmosphere, which is now more oxygen, helium and hydrogen-abundant, also contributes to the uniformity and stability of the weather across the globe – a process that gradually spans over a period of 20 to 25 years.

The Earth's new axis rotation is synchronized with the rotation cycle changes of the other planets within your solar system. Saturn and Jupiter are, in fact, the initiators of such new rotation cycle, followed by Uranus, then Pluto, then Mars, Venus, Mercury and the Earth. Neptune's shifting, on the other hand, remains seamlessly integrated within the other planets' re-positioning sequence. The rotation cycles are triggered by the energies of the newly born hexagonal grids over the north pole of each planet consecutively. This means that, in 2007, Saturn begins its new rotational cycle as soon as its axis becomes congruent with its new hexagon-shaped grid, followed by Uranus, then Jupiter, then Pluto, etc., until the new rotational ratio between all the planets of your solar system becomes congruent. On the other hand, the Earth and Moon cycles also become congruent with Mars' and then replicates this new shift with Venus, then with Mercury. This cyclical transformation establishes a system of calibration that thrusts your entire solar system into a new formation, allowing the birth of 2 new planets within your system. These 2 planets, which are yet to be named by your scientists, have been perpetually present and have been part of your solar system since it was originally conceived. It is only after the new rotational cycles and calibration systems are instilled that they become apparent to you, making the total count of your planets 12 instead of 10.[44] **See figure 23 on page 98.**

The purpose of such planetary system reconfiguration is to integrate the universal knowledge and principles within the very organisms of the individual planets. Without such a perfectly orchestrated astronomical movement and repositioning, cosmic light and universal information remain restricted to the linear reality currently in exist-

---

44   Not including the Moon.

ence on your Earth. These astronomical changes also allow the new vibration of the hexagon-shaped grids to open the shafts of light from the galactic core straight into each individual planet, creating a sudden integration of cosmic information between the worlds.

From Source's perspective, it will appear as if the Earth were upheld by a stupendously complex circuit of light beams linking it directly to the center of the galaxy and, in turn, the core of the Local Universe. This rearrangement of your planetary system within the Milky Way now positions your planet in such a way as to draw direct energy and information from the galactic center – the area of the Central Suns. This energetic opening manifests physically on Earth in a gradual manner beginning in 2012 and integrates harmonious energetic adjustments, powerful cosmic interchange, magnificent new systems of information and spectacular interplanetary transportation structures between the worlds. **See figure 19 on page 85.**

OTHER GEOPHYSICAL CHANGES ...

The process, by which the reconstructive geophysical changes on the Earth occur, is seamlessly synchronized and orchestrated. This plan has been envisioned and is currently being directed and carried out by the divine entities that are of the Creator Order – those responsible for the creation, management and instilment of planetary systems as well as the wellbeing of the intelligent life therein. It is therefore these Divine Beings who allow such creation to occur according to divine principles and laws. It is not the intent or in the nature of this Divine Order to cause fear or chaos to the children of Time and Space as these tremendous changes occur. There exists, however, a divine law to physical reality – that all creation must have a cycle in order to regenerate into a new form or a new sequence of life. It is now the purpose of the Divine Order, as well as your humanity's, to enter into its new cycle through this very renewing and rebirthing process with as much grace and dignity as possible. While many parts of the globe incur great physiological change for the purpose of this renewal, *those areas that must be salvaged in their current condition remain unharmed* throughout this shift and resurface gracefully at the time the major geophysical adjustments are complete.

The manifestation of landmass changes begins with the fissure in the Atlantic tectonic plate between the Americas and the European peninsula. This critical location of the Earth's underwater land mass contains the original formula of the eco-system and living organisms on the planet. This means that the microbial, atomic, mineral and other chemical substances that created the original eco-system on the Earth are present in the core of the planet in this location. This original eco-system formula, which complies with the divine blueprint, is propelled by the inner mechanism present at this site, creating the various landmass configurations observed throughout Earth's history. Each time the Earth becomes in danger of severe damage or extinction due to an overload of toxicity, the planet will create a new formula in this primal location and will trigger the necessary geophysical shifts to regain its inherent harmony and stability. These very shifts are currently occurring on your planet and will begin producing various forms of eruptions and movements within the core and subsequently throughout the entire planet, re-configuring the landmass according to the planet's next evolutionary cycle. This new reconfiguration allows the Earth to replenish its organs and cells as well as jumpstart, so to speak, its entire eco-system. The effects of such fissure are not only observable in the indicated regions. Rather, they trigger a chain reaction, so to speak, as they enhance the fault line that affects the Arctic Circle, creating an opening within the underwater structures and deep within the Earth's mantle. This shock to the underwater landmass and the deeper earth plates reverberates tremendously within the core of the planet and affects the Earth's main axes, causing them to shift. At this stage, the entire planetary tectonic structure is affected in all regions of the world in either a synchronized or simultaneous manner, and the actual reshaping of the planet's landmass begins.

As of 2008, great storms, triggered by the Atlantic tectonic rupture, submerge some areas in Southern and Northern Florida, Georgia, South Carolina and most of the northwestern coasts of Florida as well as the regions neighboring the Gulf of Mexico. On the other hand, the North Eastern areas of the North American continent begin to incur a gradual land slippage, affecting the areas falling north of Virginia up to the state of Maine and Nova Scotia. The irreparable damage to the landmass in these coastal regions occurs gradually and is accompanied by great storms and continuous floods, eventually submerging most of these areas with the Atlantic waters.

The geophysical events between 2009 and 2010 in the northwestern parts of the US and the adjoining Canadian areas are also some of the observable dramatic earth changes. A series of volcanic eruptions in the region bring about the necessary adjustments in the eco-system that are greatly needed by the Earth to continue sustaining a healthy existence. With such volcanic events, triggered by the corresponding tectonic breakages, the land in those regions begins to alter, gradually collapsing and allowing the waters of the Pacific to penetrate deep into the continent. Simultaneously, the areas of Southern California are affected by the sudden tectonic shifting and a series of earthquakes begins to occur. This area incurs a more gradual but nonetheless dramatic consequence, also allowing the waters of the Pacific to submerge most of the coast and deep into the southwestern areas of the North American continent.

The regions mostly affected by geophysical changes in Central America and in the South American continents are those located along the Ring of Fire, which also includes parts of Antarctica. The regions situated west of Argentina in the south and Columbia in the north are mostly struck by tremendous aftershocks, separating portions of the land from the continent entirely.

Europe also incurs sudden changes in its territorial structure, mainly affecting the regions closest to the Arctic Circle. Coastal regions are similarly submerged far-inland within the continent while new islands begin to appear and form in their stead. Other parts of Europe that are greatly affected are the northern territories of the Eastern Block, Turkey and Greece that sit on the currently known fault lines. The tectonic movement that ensues affects the uranium filled underground facilities in the regions neighboring the Caspian Sea, allowing toxic chemical to surface and engulf the region. The areas neighboring and south of the Caspian Sea also suffer great fires that devastate large portions of the lands. On the other hand, the shifting of the Indian tectonic plates also triggers breakages in the regions situated on the Indian and Pakistani border, affecting the long-drawn clashes and political organization of these 2 nations.

Asia suffers greatly from the tectonic repercussions of the Arctic Circle as the lands falling within the vicinity and north of the Sea of Japan are also submerged. Similarly, Southeast Asia – namely the area between Thailand, Australia and New Guinea – is transformed entirely by repeated powerful earthquakes and endless storms.

The geophysical changes that occur worldwide, while having tremendous consequences on all levels and in all continents, do not alter dramatically the physicality of Africa. This continent suffers, however, the dire consequence of atmospheric changes and long-drawn out droughts, starving its land and leading it to total barrenness. Australia, on the other hand, separates from the other continents, disconnecting itself further from the rest of the world. For a period of 18 to 24 months beginning in 2009, the entire planet is affected intermittently by one geophysical event or another. These events include drastic atmospheric changes – such as tremendous heat, drought or icing – prolonged power outages and electrical storms, continuous outbursts of sporadic wildfires and restricted water and food supplies. As a result, the existing governmental and other support systems are shut down due to overwhelming demand and the daily routine is inevitably halted and reassessed worldwide.

While these dramatic developments in the Earth's history do alter entirely the reality in which humanity is living, you must realize that *such a process must be regarded within the context of a Divine Plan at work.* This process of rejuvenation is necessary for the Earth to jumpstart, so to speak, its new cyclical movement. The complete shut down of the currently running systems brings the Earth's pulse and breathing patterns to a halt, allowing her to rest at zero point for a time before her newly re-calibrated cycles begin. This perfect stillness of the Earth's movements suddenly suspend the mind-al, spiritual and physical tensions of the planet and its inhabitants, creating a peculiar combination of awe and exaltation all at once. Your individual experience may therefore range from fear and anguish to delicious ecstasy or bliss depending on your focus, your intent and your courage. While this period is indeed a time of seemingly great upheaval, in fact, it is but the birthing of a brilliant new experience and the emergence of a great new generation of Love, Truth, Beauty and Goodness on the earth plane and beyond.

10

Ramifications Of The Divine Plan For The Individual

The effects of the Divine Plan are multi-dimensional and inevitable while still being created all at once. This means that the energy that is becoming available to you, while already here, is increasingly unfolding before your eyes. This new energy affects the earth plane on all levels and is indeed unavoidable. However, it is still *the choice of the individual* to experience and embrace such a phenomenon or reject participation altogether. As such, the unfolding Divine Plan, while having predictable consequences on the physical, mental, emotional and spiritual aspects of earthly life, remains a *potential and subjective* experience that each individual must *ask or intend for*. Since thought creates your physical experience, it is that which you think of, intend and ask for that comes to your attention. You may also intend to remain oblivious to an entire reality if you consciously choose to do so. However, this Divine Plan brings between the years 2008 and 2013 the culmination of accumulated dual energy, which becomes so apparent that it will be difficult to remain oblivious to it. In other words, the difference between positive and negative energy becomes so great that everyone is now able to grasp Truth in a direct and spontaneous manner. Truth is no longer concealed beneath the veils of your reality or behind the deeds of misguided leaders. In that sense, the Divine Plan makes the co-existence of divine and destructive energy impossible. A new system must and will be generated.

ELECTROMAGNETIC RAMIFICATIONS FOR THE INDIVIDUAL ...

The electromagnetic movements that occur as early as 2007, and more rapidly between 2012 and 2020, provide humanity with a way to awaken at higher speed, clearly witnessing its own essence being birthed on the earth plane. Individually, you are now able to witness firsthand your true electromagnetic frequency range as an actual beam of light that begins at your birthplace within the universal structure and ends on Earth through your actual physical apparatus. You gradually but surely witness the immensity of your being, knowing for a fact that you are simultaneously connected to other worlds through an intricate circuitry of light beams. From the perspective of your universal birthplace, you will soon be able to see the entire light beam structure that represents you and that you permanently hold, even as you manifest in human form. This tremendous awareness clearly reestablishes your identity and clarifies your need for physical incarnation, which is to implant such remarkable electromagnetic light beam formation onto the earth plane.

While it may be difficult to observe from the Earth's perspective the massiveness of your individual being, from the perspective of your birthplace you will be able to see that the entire light beam structure you carry is, in fact, in the form of an infinite geometric DNA pattern being implanted onto the Earth. Your individual awakening is the very activation of such new and massive genetic vibration, which also awakens the entire planet and humanity at greater speed and brings about the New Era of Love and Light. Once such global awakening is achieved, it also becomes reflected back to Source.

As each individual awakens to his/her own DNA pattern, s/he is able to integrate it with other co-existing patterns that are also awakening. Eventually, all DNA light beam structures fit perfectly and magnificently within a larger structure of divine DNA, which is the actual and original divine blueprint of Creator Energy – that of your Divine Creator and the Divine Source.

PHYSICAL MANIFESTATION OF THE DIVINE PLAN ...

As early as 2009, the more dramatic physical manifestations of the Divine Plan begin to appear, ranging from atmospheric and geological changes to actual physical ruptures within your current physical experience. Some of these changes do actually occur suddenly, but their effects and ramifications continue unfolding in a gradual manner over the next 200 to 300 years.

As the Earth settles in its new configuration in relation to the Sun and the galactic center, this triggers a chain of reactions that includes the spontaneous reversal of Moon cycles and the sudden appearance of new stars. These stars are not created anew but, rather, become suddenly visible to you. The Moon cycles and rotations expand in such a way as to lengthen your current calendar day, month and year, thereby redefining your chronological experience of time altogether. Similarly, your Sun also shifts in such a way as to appear "larger," allowing an entire new octave of light to become available to you. Your current human visual spectrum allows only one octave of light – out of the 100 available in your universe – to be visible, whereas this new shift expands your visible range to 2 or more octaves at once and continues expanding it exponentially thereafter. Therefore, not only is the human brain able to absorb a larger amount of light, but all geophysical life and its respective cycles are also affected.

The result of absorbing a larger or higher octave of light allows the human species to perceive reality in a new and expanded way. Other wavelengths, where Mind and Spirit Energy reside, for example, are now easily detectable, while subtle energy becomes commonly observed. The implications of such phenomenon are tremendous in the sense that they affect all of the individual's earthly experiences. Those in human form who have been elevating their consciousness steadily no longer must guess which layers of reality or "dimensions" exist within the earth plane; they are simply able to perceive them directly and accurately. While some beings open up to this experience faster than others, all are, in time, able to attain such higher levels of awareness.

The perceptual expansion of the individual also means that the actual *appearance* of the earth plane is modified. You may compare this experience with a sort of thin veil before your eyes that is suddenly lifted, allowing a clearer vision of what lies ahead. As the new energy is instilled on the earth plane, *an actual splitting of the layers of reality* – or frequency ranges - occurs that ruptures the 2 conflicting energy fields altogether. The higher frequency ranges that are aligned with Source Energy actually separate, leaving behind the lower energy fields that remain attached to the old energetic and geometric structure currently in place. Since your human perceptual experience implies that you are tuned into a 3rd-dimensional frequency range, this separation of frequencies, in fact, affects your entire perception of the reality around you. In some cases, those physical areas that remain attached to the older system - or lower frequency ranges – suddenly disappear from your perspective entirely. This sort of fissure in your visual experience includes the sudden collapse or disappearance of actual buildings or streets, making your reality a real and factual perceptual shift. While fear may arise within those who are uninformed, misguided or simply unwilling to open to the Truth surfacing on the earth plane, the emergence of the higher vibrations is, in fact, an exquisite experience, as *it is the ultimate and authentic blending and reunification with Divine Source Energy on the planet.* Your new reality and entire being are suddenly bathed in a tremendous and superb energy of Love, Light, Truth, Beauty and Goodness. All that is required is to be attuned to the highest good of self and humanity and this tremendous experience can and must only be exquisitely divine.

PHYSICAL AWAKENING TO THE DIVINE PLAN ...

As the various beings incarnated on Earth begin to awaken to their individual true essence and remember their role in the Divine Plan, they may experience what appears to be disturbances, imbalances or difficulties with their physical apparatus. These disturbances are due to the shifting of their frequency range from the human to their original one, which is attached to highly complex and powerfully charged circuits.[45] This process is gradual but necessary as it is part of the very plan they have embraced and are representing. When these individual souls awaken gradually to their original true self, they download, so to speak, these higher frequencies at a pace that still remains somewhat comfortable and tolerable. However, due to their highly sensitive nature, they may experience some discomfort at times. On one level, these discomforts contribute to the individual's own spiritual growth and mind mastery. On the other hand, these symptoms relate to the global shifts they are witnessing through their intimate energetic link with the respective planetary circuits. Some of the main symptoms or disturbances commonly observed within this magnificent group of beings[46] can be summarized as follows: head disturbances, pressure in the head, ringing in the ears, feeling of dizziness, etc., which are part of the Mind Energy adjustments and represent the planet's Mind-Body electromagnetic shift. Liver and digestive sluggishness are part of the emotional and mental bodies being detoxified from the lower frequencies. These symptoms also correspond to the severity of upcoming earthly events such as cataclysms, earthquakes, etc. Spleen imbalances are related to the creating and birthing of the new energy on the planet. Joints relate to the connectivity of the realms – physical and spiritual – as well as the relationship between the collective planetary consciousness and the stellar, galactic and universal structures. Throat blockages correspond to the collective expressive energy, such as demonstrations, riots, etc. Sinus issues represent the overflow of collective emotions that are resisting release, such as global disease or famine. Bleeding and menses problems relate to overwhelming stressful events, such as world crisis and famine. Heart and thymus gland stress, which includes tachycardia, heart murmur, pressure, etc., relates to human failures in past lives and global history as well as the integration of Spirit Energy within the physical realm. Fatigue and exhaustion relate to the tremendous amount of energy being shifted individually and globally. And finally, overall emotional imbalances such as depression or melancholy represent the actual release of old patterns as

---

45 As described in the previous chapters of this book.
46 Many other beings may also experience similar symptoms. The way to cope with such discomforts is discussed in Part III of this book.

well as the need to be aligned with Source or the desire to return to the original Home.

SPIRITUAL MANIFESTATION OF THE DIVINE PLAN ...

Along with the separation of the worlds, which begins as early as 2009, comes the sudden experience of tremendous joy vibration throughout the earth plane. It is as if the skies have suddenly opened up, releasing a spectacular blanket of love and wrapping the entire humanity with its warmth and peaceful vibration. This energy of love and joy is felt by all, but the way or process through which it is displayed may appease some while frightening others. Those accustomed to or open to the concept of divine intervention or divine presence simply delight in this tremendous energy long awaited for. But those who are skeptical may simply resent it and refuse to truly experience this powerful and uplifting new vibration.

Regardless of the individual response to this emerging global Love vibration, a spark of light is felt in everyone's heart. This is meant to allow those who are straggling along or not quite understanding the meaning or the process of such phenomenon, to gradually adjust and find their way comfortably within the layers of the new reality. Indeed *all* do see, feel and sense this spectacular energy within their entire being, regardless of age, race, spiritual level of understanding, location on the planet or previous actions. *All* are equally and completely endowed with the divine grace and love of the new Creator Energy that becomes prominently present on the Earth. For those who have long awaited this spectacular event, this shift feels like a sudden surge of light running through their being, producing instant bliss, excitement and spontaneous enlightenment. However, those who are truly cognizant of the Divine Plan but choose to continue isolating themselves from Source and deliberately harming others inevitably remain sequestered in the lower frequencies of the earth plane and gradually dissolve within their own reality. And those who are somewhat in between, unable to understand the process and feel trapped or lost along the way, are assisted by their loving spirit guardians who will most certainly usher them to their safety and salvation.

Globally, a sudden sense of belonging and unification surfaces among the different spiritual schools of thought and institutions. This is a gradual process, however, that develops over a period of 22 years – from 2013 onward – and culminates in the obliteration of all discriminating religious sects. At that time only does a new unifying form of spirituality arise, bringing the world to a new understanding of "God." You may say that by 2035 the traditional religions you know on the planet now are abolished, making way for a new spiritual understanding based on the Law of One, which is a truthful and unified planetary alignment with the One Divine Source of the Local Universe.

EMOTIONAL MANIFESTATIONS OF THE DIVINE PLAN ...

As the higher frequencies of the Divine Plan make their appearance on the earth plane, the human sensory perception system is altered. The human senses become more acute, more precise and more evolved. In time, the human senses also become joined in such a way as to create a new way of perceiving reality altogether and thus interacting with and reacting to it. So far, human emotions have been the cause of confusion, misleading you in your decision making. Now, your emotions become clearer as to surface only when necessary, so to speak. The emotional blocks accumulated through the years seem to suddenly untangle and work in harmony with the mind. Such a process affects the individual in various degrees. However, the ability to sustain an overall emotional balance is now certainly present among those open to the arrival of the New Era. On the other hand, individuals who persistently cling onto the lower vibrations may not allow such clarity and freedom from emotional imbalance. In fact, this movement and energy shift may enhance further their entangled emotional field, leading them to more grief and even despair.

MIND-AL MANIFESTATION OF THE DIVINE PLAN …

As the human minds begin to align with the Divine Mind of the Source, a sudden awareness of the divine self appears within each individual, making the mind clearer, freer and more expanded. At once, there are those who may see and understand truth from a more evolved perspective, while others may still suffer sudden mental imbalance. Once more, your experience depends upon the frequencies into which you are tuned. Even those who are unaware of such changes or are unable to understand the process do automatically shift to the higher vibrations by default, so to speak, thereby experiencing a sudden clarity of thought.

The human mind also begins to accelerate so as to process information in a rapid and accurate manner. This accelerated new mind acts in accordance with divine principles that allow the retrieval of global and universal information in a more precise and speedy manner. The newly re-aligned mind channels become a superior means for higher knowledge and truth and allow clearer discernment of the various realities. Your mind simply becomes a superb operating tool, leading you to higher cognitive, intellectual and spiritual functioning not yet experienced on this Earth. The exquisite blend of cognitive ability with a true sense of unified spirituality becomes the basis for the New Era and the new birthed species on the Earth.

11

Unification Of The Spiritual Trends

Religious beliefs are as ancient as the appearance of man on Earth. It is imperative for humans to create a belief system in which they can function that justifies the supernatural and those inexplicable universal laws that govern the physical realms. Through time, the definition of God, the mysteries of Creation and the nature of physical reality have been modified countless times in order to satisfy the needs of the society and era in question. Similarly, with the current energetic shifts occurring on the earth plane, a new concept of religion and spirituality must also surface.

The emergence of a new spirituality has been facilitated for the past decades by the Truth aspect of the Creator Energy surfacing on the earth plane. The momentum of Truth has now accelerated enough as to instigate a surge of new information that had been sealed from human consciousness for millennia at a time. Even though most of your current main religions have been based on Truth, the human *interpretation* of such Truth has created a distorted and conflicting understanding of true spirituality on Earth. The appearance of new revelations and spiritual beliefs has certainly occurred periodically within the human realm. However, it is only now that the shortcomings of your churches, temples and shrines are becoming bluntly and globally apparent all at once. It is today commonplace to find religious advocates involved in devious activity or engaged in worldwide violence in the name of "God." Such tremendous distortions of true religion have now, more than even before, divided public opinion and confused the public's perception and feelings about a true and loving religion.

The manifestation of the new emerging spirituality supports each individual's own *direct connection* to the Divine Creator. By nature, humans feel the need to learn from others through teachings or through holy books written by yet other humans. What we now see occurring is the search for validity in those unquestioned revelations from holy books, upon which humanity has blindly based its faith and traditions. With time, these unquestioned revelations become obsolete as they clearly foster division, competitiveness and separation between the various sects. Soon enough, your current religions, because they do not support a unified world based on true spiritual oneness with Creator, become obsolete. As such, your individual *clarity regarding your own true essence*, supported by a new expanded *perception of reality*, now enables you to effortlessly establish a clear and direct link between yourself – in physical form – and Creator. Such is the power of the New Era, when each and every individual requires nothing but his/her own self to experience the link between physicality and spirituality, between physical life on Earth and reality in Spirit. Such is the ultimate blending of the Mind, Spirit and Physical realms through the recognition of your own divinity and spiritual power.

THE TRANSITION TO UNIFIED SPIRITUALITY ...

The transition, from your current established religions to the unified spirituality trend of the New Era, is facilitated by many critical shifts in the various arenas – political, socio-economical, educational and racial. Beginning in the year 2000 and escalating to 2012, political clashes and wars waged in the name of religion, which lead to continuous and unnecessary bloodshed and human suffering, bring such acts into the awareness of the entire globe, causing demand that such actions be banned from the established religions altogether. These worldly clashes, based on distorted religious principles as well as group action court cases, become the target of criticism and division within the different sects, further separating and dismantling the basic religious structures currently in existence. This disintegration occurs violently at first but eventually settles into new agreements, where each separate party forms new institutional alliances and representations. This is the process by which the current main religions become smaller and less effective. Once the dismantling occurs, the Earth, now in the process of uniting, calls for a reassembly of those smaller and divided sects that have left its members confused and perplexed. Along with the individual's own consciousness expansion, a global need for the Truth brings the spiritual trends together into a new authentic relationship with Creator or "God." The New Era of spirituality, which truly begins in 2035, brings a new alignment of faiths and allows for all to share the truthful knowledge and understanding of humanity's relationship with Creator. While unified in this universal faith, each individual remains responsible for caring for his/her own approach and practice of such truth and faith. Your current churches, temples and shrines make room for new domes and divine geometry structures for social congregations. In these divine structures, the individual's participation is based on humility and the love for his/her own divinity, the honoring of his/her physicality and the Divine Order in general. These gatherings are of utmost splendor as all become focused on one universal principle based on Love, Truth, Beauty and Goodness for every living human being on planet Earth, bypassing all cultural, racial or sexual differences at once. This indeed is the ultimate realization of "God" while in the flesh – a unified call, yet unique to each individual's character and personality.

By mid-century, the newly formed unified spirituality is clearly shaped. Prayers become somewhat universal, supporting the spirit of the individual's intent, the planet as a whole, its connection to its galactic neighbors and its direct link to Source. While each individual may still choose to express such prayers in his/her own way, the general focus of such prayer becomes universal and makes each individual a family member of the entire humanity. This powerful spiritual change, once instilled, cannot be reversed or dismantled as it offers true freedom and support for the new enlightened individual's belief system and becomes simultaneously supported by the emerging political, socio-economical, astronomical and others major energetic shifts that occur within that time. The New Spirituality is based on an exquisite blend of Truth, cosmology, a new form of mathematics, divine geometry and physics and ultimately moves humanity towards a unified and loving species. The beliefs of the New Spirituality may be summarized as follows:

1. All intelligent beings are created through Mind Energy by the First Source, a Divine Father and Divine Mother, located at the center of your local universe. Each created being is endowed with a similar and equal link to the Divine Creator and Source. Therefore, all are capable of attaining self-realization and direct contact with Source.

2. All existence is Energy, which manifests in infinite Mind-al, Spiritual and Physical forms. Since energy has an inherent electromagnetic vibration, it is perpetually interrelated with all aspects of Creation. The physical worlds are therefore the extension of the divine realms and share the same infinite properties and principles of Love, Truth, Beauty and Goodness.

3. It is the individual's choice to incarnate in human form for the purpose of learning to master dimensionality, experience creativity within a physical realm and expand his/her consciousness. At the time of incarnation, each being partakes in an individual experience as well as a collective Mind-Spirit-Body matrix. Therefore, each individual is responsible for his/her own reality while also automatically contributing to the collective human consciousness matrix.

4. Prior to physical incarnation, it is the individual's choice to create an agreement with him/herself and Creator regarding the need and purpose of said incarnation. However, once in physical form, the individual must manifest such an agreement as s/he goes along. This physical manifestation

occurs through Mind Energy or Thought. Therefore, Thought is the fuel of creation and materialization. Thought attracts its vibrational match – positive thought attracts a positive outcome whereas negative thought attracts a negative outcome. However, materializing or manifesting a thought, prayer or intent is dependent upon the conscious alignment with your belief systems as well as the human creative formula, which includes: thought, desire,[47] belief and detachment.

5. While spiritual gatherings may still be appropriate and beneficial at times, connection to Creator and actual prayer occur through the personal and direct invocation of the Divine Source and the alignment of your individual physical self with Source, without any human or spirit intermediaries.[48] While others may facilitate the process of such invocation, this form of prayer spontaneously raises your own individual vibration and allows an automatic merging with your own Spirit Self – higher consciousness – and Spirit Family in a direct unobstructed manner. The way to express such prayer – as well as the location and frequency of this prayer – is subjective to the individual's lifestyle and unique taste.

6. There are no observed traditions for the new spirituality other than consecrating time daily for the contemplation of your divine essence and direct communion with the divine worlds. This new form of honoring and respecting the divine order and your own divinity become integrated in your daily life, workplace, social circle and earthly career. You are continuously guided to upkeep your physical apparatus with utmost dignity, gratitude and love, which is then automatically reflected through your interactions within your home, family unit as well as with nature, the animal kingdom and the plant and mineral life.

7. The concepts of marriage and family remain subject to the individual's own choice and earthly purpose, while the breeding of offspring is now based on global awareness

---

47 Will of the individual.
48 Intermediaries include priests, rabbis, shamans, gurus, saints, etc., other beings such as animals or man-made objects and instruments.

and the honoring of and respect for a harmonious collective earthly existence.

8. The recognition and full comprehension of the invisible divine government are essential for the deliberate manifestation of higher consciousness and the evolution of species on the physical plane. This awareness also redefines the true meaning of the concept "As above so below" and allows the replication of such divine concepts within the human realm.

12

Government And Consciousness

Between 2000 and 2012, there is a noted arising need for Truth. The emergence of the new Creator Energy on Earth increasingly triggers such events as political scandals, significant court cases and the uprising of the people in demand for Truth. While such events have happened at other times in Earth's history, the events between the years 2000 and 2012 form a steady and accelerated means by which Truth is unveiled on a global scale. Africa's devastating crime, famine and disease and other countries' despotic regimes are but a few examples of this emerging Truth – regarding inadequate governmental functioning worldwide. The accelerated momentum of unveiled governmental cover-ups and deceitful corporate behaviors begins to alter the individual's perception of what government is or should be. This wake-up call is further triggered by catastrophes such as natural disasters or the threats of war, for example, blatantly revealing the incompetence and the highly bureaucratic but inefficient systems currently in place. The magnitude of such events naturally entices the individual to question the validity of current governmental policies, which forces the current structure into change.

While some areas of the globe must go through a rough transition due to the momentum they have already accumulated, others shift into the New Era with much grace and synchronization. The areas of the Middle East, for example, namely Israel and the Arab world; India and Pakistan; China; the United States and North Korea, maintain their focus on military power play, and conflicts escalate dramatically commencing in 2006. However, by the years 2009 and 2010, the global governmental and economic clashes are halted due to the significant electromagnetic shifts – namely, the polar shift and subsequent geophysical adjustments – and the work of rebuilding a new world based on just and truthful governments begins. The emerging new energies that affect the physical, mental, emotional and spiritual aspects of the individual, combined with the observed global traumas, trigger an overall awareness of governmental shortfalls worldwide.

Beginning in 2007 and more markedly after 2013, an awakened global consciousness surfaces upon the Earth. While this shift has already begun, this is the beginning of a *real* re-organization of governmental structures worldwide. Due to extensive military involvement, the internal structure of superpower states suffers tremendously, literally splitting the countries into fragments. Those involved in governmental duties, in the US and other superpowers, begin to realize the magnitude of their work as it pertains not only to their individual state but also to the Earth altogether. This surge of tremendous responsibility produces a rapid shake up in governments across the globe, pressuring those in office who are incapable of fulfilling global demands in truth and honesty to step down and vacate their posts. Simultaneously, those humans who are fully aware of the Divine Plan and their role in the shift begin to fill these new posts and assist in the creation of the New Era. The sudden collapse in the governments of superpower states initiates a chain reaction, so to speak, summoning a global re-organization and the creation of a highly evolved and functioning system. Between the years of 2013 and 2035, the re-organization of the governments around the world takes place. This is a most anticipated and unprecedented event as this extraordinary period practically becomes the backbone of the New Era on the planet and within the planetary system.

CONSCIOUSNESS AND THE CREATION OF A NEW GOVERNMENT ...

As the consciousness of the individual expands, the layers of reality that have been thus far inaccessible or sealed begin to unlock. Your sudden expanded perception of the earth plane, the galactic structure and the universal organization creates a new and clear experience of the physical world and allows you to reach others on the globe and in other layers of reality with ease and clarity. You are now able to have *direct contact* with new realities beyond the 3rd dimension and instantly recognize your citizenship within a wider universal organization – not only planetary but also inter-planetary and galactic all at once. This direct and spontaneous recognition allows no room for error or misinterpretation as each of you is now participating in a new experience where you are the prime and direct observer of Truth.

While chaos may erupt in certain regions of the globe, the simultaneous emergence of the sentient beings involved in the Divine Plan makes this transition gradual, natural, effective and balanced in many ways. The new, emerging vibrations suddenly create a sense of reality that is pleasing, peaceful and loving – a global reality so far unknown to man on Earth. It is as if your air and space become filled with enlightened energy, triggering an immediate awakening of the global mind and spirit – a significant event awaited by many at this moment in time. While this transition may appear disturbing to some, it is, in fact, in accordance with the divine principles and will lovingly overshadow your fears and qualms. It simply unfolds as a spectacular *blanket of love* wrapping around the Earth an overwhelming feeling of serenity and peace.

The way by which such magnificent change occurs is through the work of the incarnate Divine Father – and Divine Son – in human form. As He awakens to His own essence, He automatically begins to realize the importance of His work and effect on global consciousness. By directing His enlightened focus to the political leaders currently in place, He is able to neutralize many of these leaders' offensive behaviors, transmuting their deeds into light energy aligned with Source and this is precisely the reason for the incarnation of this magnificent being in human form!

Note

The following chapter is intended to inspire the new generation to envision and create a world based on Universal Love. This new system allows the replication on Earth of the divine concepts instilled in the Higher Realms, thereby redefining the true meaning of "As above, so below!"

13

The New Government On Earth

Within the next 12 to 15 years, the idea of a universal government emerges. It is now up to the enlightened species to dictate how their individual state must fit into the entire scheme of human consciousness. It is now up to those who have truly awakened to their divinity and alignment to set the tone, so to speak, for a new form of government that functions in peace with the neighboring worlds and within a cohesive galactic and universal structure. While the actual implementation of such grand plan may take up to mid-century, humanity in unison shall now agree on the new grounds of an earth government that is based on Love, Truth, Beauty and Goodness.

The following is a simplified model of a universal governmental agreement that supports *all nations alike.* This sample agreement, which begins to surface on the earth plane within a few years following 2012, becomes practically established by mid-century and is based on the following universal intent: "We the people of this Earth ask and intend to create and thus ordain one universal agreement and government based on Love, Truth, Beauty and Goodness for *all countries equally*, for the purpose of co-existing in a peaceful, abundant and just world. As such, *all members of such government shall be fully awakened and aware of their universal citizenship and divine lineage.* The individual countries within this unified earth government shall have similar political offices and posts, which represent the needs of the people and shall encompass respective ministries as follows:

OFFICE OF THE PRESIDENTS:

While each country continues to hold its own presidential office, these nominated candidates also represent their respective country within a planetary presidential organization that services the entire globe. This planetary office is formed by 2 presidents – one nominee of each sex – who are elected by the presidents of all countries. The presidents' tasks encompass the proper operation and functioning of all other offices described below. In case one of the presidents becomes deceased prior to the termination of term, a new president shall be elected in his/her place to complete the remainder of the term.

OFFICE OF THE CHIEF EXECUTIVES:

There are 2 planetary chief executives who supply the Office of the Presidents with the needed support. All chief executives are required to have served as a member of 3 other offices for a minimum period of 7 years combined, which acquaints them with and prepares them for such a demanding and important post. The chief executives are elected by the people of the individual countries with the approval of the elected presidents. Their main focus and work is to create a transparent and cohesive liaison between the Office of the Presidents, the other ministries and the people. It is their main duty to interact with all the heads of the various offices and insure proper functioning within each. They preside over the court system and judicial affairs of the presidents and lead the official meetings accordingly.

OFFICE OF THE GENERAL ASSEMBLY:

The Office of the General Assembly is in charge of planetary judicial affairs, represents all countries and acts as a sort of Supreme Court. This office, which is comprised of 24 members elected by the Presidents and the Chief Executives, is also supported by the people. This means that if a member of this court does not represent adequately the judicial needs of the people, that member may be removed and replaced automatically through a specialized ballot system.

This assembly's primary focus is to implement the laws passed and approved by the Offices of the Presidents and Chief Executives. While it may at first still proceed with the current punishment laws regarding destructive human enactment, this assembly eventually transitions into the areas of general law implementation as the human spirit also transitions into a more peaceful and enlightened species. At all times, the Office of the General Assembly shall apply laws within the material worlds that are based on the divine principles.

OFFICE OF MONETARY DISTRIBUTION AND BARTER:

The Office of Monetary Distribution and Barter comprises 100 members and is headed by 12 members who are elected by the people. This office controls the proper flow of monetary exchange and material barter between nations to insure that they have been properly allocated. It is now up to each country individually and the Earth collectively to insure that the needs of all people regarding energy, food and water are adequately met. This office does not interfere with the affairs of the individual but rather directs the monies gained through taxes to the appropriate parties. The current monetary system becomes greatly refined and altered through this tremendous Earth transition, and, with the rise of global planetary consciousness, the monetary system is gradually and efficiently replaced with pure barter of material goods. This newly emerging system does not hinder the human ambition or desire for prosperity. Quite the contrary, it provides a greater impetus for the human soul, which is now directed towards the achievement of grand cosmic ideas and the creation of new realities of greater proportion that may still be unimaginable to you now.

THE MINISTRY OF TAXES:

The Ministry of Taxes is comprised of 10 main officers and several hundred office members within each state and is in charge of collecting government taxes from each citizen within their respective country. The 10 main officers are elected by the people and supervised by the Chief Executives. The new system takes up to mid-century to fully adjust and balance the needs of the entire population. Eventually, this new program involves the collection of a uniform 10% of the individual's income regardless of their accumulated assets or earnings. While the actual allocation of the collected taxes is not part of this ministry's duties, it is important to note that these collected funds are to be utilized for the creation of public systems, such as transportation, roads, buildings, energy and water distribution systems, etc. The current spending for such items as wars, military equipments, and health insurance, among others, gradually becomes obsolete.

THE MINISTRY OF NEW SCIENCE:
 The Ministry of New Science is headed by highly evolved and sentient beings from all areas of science: astrophysics, new mathematics, cosmology, molecular biology, etc. Each area is represented by 3 head scientists who are experts in their field. These head scientists are also in charge of a team of 24 support scientists who continuously work for the betterment of life on Earth. With the arrival of the new consciousness, your head scientists integrate a deeper level of awareness and thus accept the creation principles as the base of their research. The work of the Ministry of New Science is now based on the multi-dimensionality of life on Earth and the probability of a Creator-Source, which infers the existence of Mind Energy and Consciousness as the true originator of an infinite physical life. Science soon becomes an exquisite blend of new mathematics and divine geometry analysis mixed with brilliant spiritual rationality.

THE MINISTRY OF ARTS AND CULTURE:
 The Ministry of Arts and Culture focuses on the proper expression of human truth and creativity through the artistic domain. This office prevents the alteration of or deviation from universal truths and refines and enhances individual artistic expression into a more sophisticated style. This ministry is also responsible for cultural exchanges between the individual countries, allowing the attributes of Beauty and Goodness to be brought forth continuously through advanced creativity and the arts. This office is headed by 2 ministers and a team of 12 members from each country who represent the programs of each nation respectively.

THE MINISTRY OF COSMIC COMMUNICATION:

The Ministry of Cosmic Communication is an important liaison between the different nations of the planet as well as the galactic neighbors and universal government. The newly established communication systems become uniform in the sense that the same principles of information distribution that are applied between the nations on Earth are also applied beyond the planet. This new system is based on pure hydrogen shafts that transport information at the speed of light from one area of the globe to another and from one center of the Earth to its neighboring worlds. This information distribution system is a replica of what is already instilled at Source, namely the method of the Sea of Glass.[49] This is a flawless communication system that not only transcends the barrier of various languages and ways of communicating among the worlds, but it also establishes a clear link that cannot be tampered with. Earthly, intergalactic and trans-universal communication is now public information, while deliberate deceit and public misguidance become obsolete.

The Ministry of Communication is divided into 3 departments: earthly, galactic and universal. Each department is segregated according to its own needs but all share the same responsibility, which is to transfer truthful information throughout the planet and beyond. Each department of this ministry is headed by 3 Prime Ministers and includes 33 members.

OFFICE OF THE EARTH GOVERNMENT AMBASSADORS:

This office comprises 200 members and represents each earth country within the Galactic Federation Organization. This office's members are elected by each country and represent the matters and affairs of the entire earth government collectively. 12 main speakers, selected by the members of this office and approved by the Offices of the Presidents and Chief Executives of each country, preside over the Office of the Earth Government Ambassadors. This Office interacts with its galactic neighbors through the reflectivity system of the Sea of Glass, as such is the universal communication system of all physical worlds and planetary systems.

---

49   See details on page ....

THE MINISTRY OF WORLD TRANSPORTATION:

The Ministry of World Transportation comprises 3 departments: earthly, galactic and universal. Each department is headed by 3 head engineers and a team of 24 head technicians who represent the global needs. This ministry is in charge of monitoring the production of computerized machinery that gives access to safe road transfers and that remain aligned with the energetic balance of the planet. No transportation device shall be utilized that does not fit within the creation principles and does not safeguard the chemical balance of the Earth. The Ministry of World Transportation also monitors interplanetary travel and is in charge of restoring and maintaining the proper functioning of all axes and grid systems within the earth plane – and beyond – that allow light body travel. These ministry officers are physically located at specified Earth locations that contain critical travel vortices between the worlds and work closely with the semi-material Divine Sons stationed at the earth grid, planetary system grid and galactic grid.

THE MINISTRY OF HIGHER EDUCATION:

The Ministry of Higher Education involves the creation and implementation of an entirely new approach to the education of children. The regimented and punitive approaches give way to an evolved process that allows the individual to tap into global information at a young age. The new educational system specializes in the area of new science, communication, cosmology, artistic expression and new spirituality in exquisitely advanced programs that enhance children's cognitive abilities to their maximum potential. This system is also supported by the newly-emerged energy that utilizes advanced technology, which transfers the information etherically rather than through the use of text or traditional language. These future devices are light and sound-based and work in unison with the new forms of energy that become abundant on the planet through the arrival of the First Temple.

This ministry is headed by 7 head professors who work in unison with 12 representatives and other aids from each nation, making this ministry over 250 members. Their posts are interchangeable in terms of subjects or subdivisions and last a period of 3 years. At the end of such a term, each member can be reelected up to 3 times in a new area of expertise.

THE MINISTRY OF AGRICULTURE:
The Ministry of Agriculture organizes the proper ways to utilize the Earth's mineral life for nutrition and to preserve its natural chemistry and energetic balance. All agricultural techniques are now required to abide by the same laws of natural preservation and cultivation. The new technologies utilized to fertilize or cultivate the Earth are based on environmentally safe hydrogen-based energy so that crops are preserved naturally from the time of cultivation to the time of consumption. This ministry is comprised of 24 members who represent groups of all nations equally.

THE MINISTRY OF THE ENVIRONMENT AND NATURAL RESOURCES:
The Ministry of the Environment is concerned with the planning, generating and upkeep of natural resources that preserve the planet's environment and eco-system. This crucial office, comprised of 24 lead scientists in varied specialties, passes laws and regulations that all individual countries must comply with in order to safeguard the proper functioning and usage of the earth natural resources and energetic supplies. Beginning in 2013, the Earth gradually transitions from its current procedures for producing and harnessing energy to a variety of temporary solutions that alleviate the tremendous burden of environmental pollution on the Earth and its atmosphere. These temporary and somewhat ineffective solutions eventually make way to an ultimate and proper way to interact with the Earth's riches and benefit fully from its inherent intelligence. Such a process requires many creative inventions and a pioneering spirit from the individual citizens – rather than any currently operating government. Nearing 2020, an economical way to harness hydrogen and fuel *the entire planet* emerges, producing abundant self-renewable energy, abundant purified water and profuse nutrition worldwide. It is at this point in history that your current reality truly becomes extraordinarily different and exquisitely evolved as the basic needs of all people are

sufficiently met and the creative focus of your world advances exponentially.

THE MINISTRY OF ANIMAL LIFE:

The Ministry of Animal Life is comprised of 12 cabinet members and several sub-officers who represent all nations. This ministry is concerned with the safeguard and proper handling of the animal species. The extraordinary environmental changes and the evolution of human consciousness that take place within the next 35 to 70 years simultaneously affect the evolution of the animal species' consciousness. Gradually, the species that no longer fit the new atmospheric shifts dissipate, while the species that survive become naturally tamer, so to speak. The new animal species that surfaces blends beautifully with the updated eco-system and atmosphere. This species continues to monitor and support the new Earth's pulse and breathing patterns. The energetic exchange between the Earth and humanity now allows animals to harmoniously co-inhabit the planet and provide much joy through energetic exchange, wholesome play and exceptional companionship. Animal abuse becomes a thing of the past along with animal consumption, which is dramatically reduced to negligible amounts before vanishing completely from humanity's consciousness.

THE MINISTRY OF MINERAL AND PLANT LIFE:

The Ministry of Mineral and Plant Life collaborates intimately with the Ministry of Environment, the Ministry of Agriculture and the Ministry of Animal Life. The Ministry of Mineral and Plant Life is comprised of 12 cabinet members who are responsible for the management, upkeep and preservation of land. These officers serve to sustain reasonable amounts of crops to feed an entire generation plentifully and evenly throughout the globe. Along with the emerging global awareness, minerals and plants are recognized as the true gems and riches of life on Earth that sustain a thriving eco-system. They serve to nourish the physical body and are used for occasional medicinal purposes. The purpose of this office is to sustain the natural mineral needs of the planet and preserve Earth's own self-renewable chemical and electrical processes and systems.

THE MINISTRY OF GALACTIC AND UNIVERSAL AFFAIRS:

The Ministry of Galactic and Universal Affairs is comprised of 100 Earth members and is headed by 12 leaders. This ministry represents the general affairs of Earth, which pertains to cosmic organization and alignment and the way in which Earth interferes with and affects other adjoining worlds in all areas, such as government, science, communication, education or spirituality. This office's primary concern is to follow and maintain the guidelines provided by the galactic and universal committees regarding the standard procedures for managing a planetary world. This ministry is needed to further enhance the knowledge of galactic and universal citizenship, while allowing Earth to participate and contribute in inter-galactic and trans-universal forums and conventions. The officers of this ministry are the true earth ambassadors and work in unison with all other offices in place.

THE MINISTRY OF JUSTICE:

The Ministry of Justice does not only refer to laws regarding destructive human enactment but to the actual manifestation of law as it pertains to life and existence in human form. This primal judicial corps is, once more, representative of the entire Earth and is comprised of 7 highly evolved sentient beings of the Divine Order. These beings represent the majority of nations that are required to adjust their population growth to the standard procedures of life-implanting on a given wholesome planetary world. While it is the individual's choice to have offspring, the laws of your new world dictate that such an act be coherent with the human evolutionary needs, which are to maintain a balance between human, animal and plant life. When such requirements are observed, the species automatically continues to evolve and create a superior race, as its basic needs are being met and integrated within a cosmically balanced system.

THE MINISTRY OF TRADE:

The Ministry of Trade comprises all of Earth's economic values and needs in terms of material and product exchange. While the Earth is moving into a new era of enlightenment, the laws of trade become more simplified, reflecting the true needs of earthly existence rather than the erratic and superfluous trade trends of unnecessary goods. This ministry is comprised of 24 members who represent all countries. The Ministry of Trade regulates the amount of exchanges being produced by one country over another in order to consistently and evenly distribute humanity's basic needs worldwide. This ministry poses laws that implement holistic living and banishes products that are disagreeable or incoherent with the natural laws. For example, electronics, clothing articles, food items or machinery that utilize power systems detrimental to the earth structure or the physical body simply vanish. They are swiftly replaced by those items that sustain intelligent communication and are based on sound and coherent hydrogen-powered systems.

THE MINISTRY OF LABOR:
The Ministry of Labor is responsible for sponsoring and overseeing equal opportunities in the area of labor and employment for all humans regardless of race, sex or prior country citizenship. Since humanity's needs are met universally and the economics of the various countries are more unified and evenly distributed, outsourcing or restricting employment to certain individuals within certain nations no longer poses a threat to society. Quite the contrary, the new labor laws facilitate humanity's embrace of global citizenship, unified prosperity and everlasting peace. The Ministry of Labor consists of 24 members who represent all nations equally.

THE MINISTRY OF HEALTH:
The Ministry of Health is comprised of 12 head scientists who are specialized in different areas of health. This office works intimately with the Ministry of Science and contributes to the evolvement of scientific research and information pertaining to the use of products that better human life. The Ministry of Health regulates and restricts the use of pharmaceuticals to extreme cases of accidents and surgery. At the same time, it enhances the profusion of natural products and non-invasive services that are based on the infrastructure of the human mind, body and spirit. Within 2 Earth cycles – or by the end of the century – physical illness becomes a thing of the past and the emerging understanding of physical health is more integral, multi-dimensional and global rather than individually-focused or symptom-

oriented. The Ministry of Health also works closely with the Ministry of Education to educate young children about their physical bodies so that their perception of physical illness is altered at an early age. This ultimately creates a joyful, self-controlled and disease-free society.

THE MINISTRY OF PEACE AND STABILITY:
The Ministry of Peace and Stability replaces your current Ministry of Defense so long as there is no need to further engage in wars against one another. This primary ministry is not localized but acts as a gerent of all countries' military. It is stationed in various earth locales at once and monitors the military activities of the world from within these strategically dispersed posts. While the need to wage war against another nation diminishes with the emergence of the new energies on the planet, there is increasing need to maintain peaceful efforts around the globe for a time. Since many nations have concurrently utilized and manufactured nuclear weaponry that can incur great damage to the planet, it is the task of this office to supervise the deployment of such existing artillery until all danger of exploitation is permanently removed. This gradual transition takes from 30 to 100 years as the world naturally merges into one cohesive body and intelligence. The Ministry of Peace is comprised of 12 head officers and several sub-offices, encompassing over 300 hundred posts.

THE MINISTRY OF HOUSING AND ARCHITECTURE:
The Ministry of Housing and Architecture is comprised of 200 members worldwide, but it is represented within this earth government by 24 outstanding engineers and architects who fully understand and apply the laws of divine geometry in the restoration of the current edifices and roads as well as the creation of the new ones. The primary focus of these ingenious, highly sophisticated and evolved sentient beings is to utilize all available resources and earth products that are aligned with self-sustainable energy and create a safe, effective, economical form of housing that is accessible to all humans on Earth. The principles involved in this work include alignment of the actual physical construction with divine geometry distribution within the earth plane as well as the galactic alignment and positioning. For

example, the roads or bridges are aligned with the distance of the planets within the solar system and their ratio of cyclical movement. The fabrics utilized for the actual buildings, on the other hand, are derived from self-sustained energy and are positioned according to the divine geometry principles of the new earth grid proportions as these proportions relate to that particular area of the Earth. This sort of intelligent construction allows all cities to be accessed and interconnected electromagnetically and electronically – through harmless hydrogen-based self-renewable energy – which swiftly replaces the old and limited infrastructures currently in place with a magnificently evolved society and lifestyle.

THE MINISTRY OF MEDIA AND PUBLIC RELATIONS:
This ministry is responsible for broadcasting information globally in a unified, non-partial manner for the purpose of sharing news and developments within each state and worldwide. The access to such information becomes uniform and transparent, while the way of broadcasting such events becomes highly technically evolved, allowing the use of planetary electro-magnetism to reach the entire world through a unified channel of communication. This creative infrastructure provides a clear and truthful system that remains untainted or spoiled, since it is aligned with all frequencies available on the entire planet at once. This transparent broadcasting system reflects the magnitude of humanity's involvement in shaping its own future and creating new structures that comply with its growth and evolution. This system also allows an impeccable distribution of information within the planet as well as within the solar and galactic systems. As with other technology, this advanced communication system is based on hydraulic infrastructures that comply with the general demands of renewable energy. This office is held by 12 primary secretaries and has several sub-offices and branches.

THE MINISTRY OF SPORTS AND ENTERTAINMENT:
The Ministry of Sports and Entertainment strives to upkeep the spirit of an evolved society by creating ingenious programs that continuously enhance higher creativity, healthy competition and sophisticated artistic advancement. The 12 main officers in charge of this

ministry represent the arts and sports advocates of each country and assist in maintaining the highest global standards while respecting free artistic expression within each state. However, the new enlightenment era is characterized by an aspiration for higher truth that is integrated in all sports activities and artistic projects. As such, sports figures and activities are no longer supported or sponsored by material trades or goods, but rather they are now focused on inspiring youngsters to master and enhance their physical body's potential, in conjunction with mind and spirit, in one area of sporting or artistic expression or another. The arts focus on enhancing the principles of Love, Truth, Beauty and Goodness as the lower human vibrations such as excessive lust, abuse or violence gradually become repugnant to this new and highly evolved society. The sports and arts forums become directed towards global friendship and truthful camaraderie and enhance Earth's potential to grow intellectually, spiritually and cosmically.

THE MINISTRY OF COSMOLOGY:
The Ministry of Cosmology is comprised of 30 scientists, physicists and cosmologists who have realized their global citizenship not only within the Earth but also within the galactic and universal structure. They enhance and create a complete new understanding and approach to cosmology as they comprehend fully Earth's new positioning and movement within the solar system and galaxy. These shifts create a new way of interacting with other intelligences on neighboring planets and those in the far-flung universe. Exciting new discoveries of planets and stars further clarify the need to include Mind, Spirit and Physical Energy in the exploration and understanding of the physical aspects of the cosmos. Science in general and cosmology in particular are no longer able to separate themselves from the larger context of Mind-Spirit-Creator Energy and begin to integrate multi-dimensionality, infinite reality and probability within the context of this seemingly finite but magnificent discipline.

THE MINISTRY OF NEW SPIRITUALITY:
The Ministry of New Spirituality strives to solidify, through spiritual beliefs, the ties between all humans. While it does not interfere

with the way in which each individual or each society practices such beliefs, this ministry does profess allegiance to common universal and spiritual laws that respect Earth's citizens within a larger galactic and universal structure. This ministry operates and is sustained by and through the same spiritual principles.[50] The Ministry of New Spirituality is no longer like Earth's current organized religious systems, which hold traditions based on the worship of one invisible and unattainable God. Rather, the new spirituality becomes a unique creative endeavor of the Mind and Spirit combined with an exquisite understanding of new mathematics, divine geometry and cosmology. This ministry allows and sustains such beliefs and expression in a diversified yet unified manner, bringing the world together towards spiritual and mind-al expansion of consciousness and race evolution. This office is headed by 7 fully awakened ministers of the highest Divine Order and represents 12 additional office members from all nations equally.

---

50 Refer to chapter 11 for more details.

Part III

Preparing for the Inevitable Change: Practical Tools

14

Basic Guidelines For The Upcoming Changes

During the imminent physical and energetic changes on this Earth, it is important that you rely on simple guidelines that direct you towards finding immediate balance and peace. The following exercises are simple and straightforward yet universally efficient and complete. This means that regardless of your age, race, religion, spiritual understanding, psychic ability or intuitive skills, your meditation style, the language you speak or the cultural, social and economical background in which you may have been brought up, performing these simple steps insures your immediate alignment with Source Enorgy. While these exercises should be performed daily, they are particularly useful during times of utmost upheaval and require but a few minutes of your time and focus. The effects of these exercises can range from an immediate sense of grounding, balance, relaxation and peace to utter joy, clear guidance from your spirit self and the full blending with higher divine energy. As you begin to practice these exercises, please remember that regardless of your individual sensitivity – whether you feel, see, sense the immediate effects of these exercises or not – they are nonetheless achieving their purpose, which is to *raise your vibration instantly* and *align your energy with the highest and purest energy form possible on Earth*. A level of trust and allowing is helpful to maximize these delicious experiences.

All exercises should be performed sitting up in a comfortable chair with your feet flat on the floor and your arms loosely resting on your thighs. Your feet contact with the floor provides a way to anchor divine energy through your crown – the top of your head – into your physical body and into the Earth beneath you. You may tape the information and play it back or simply use the CD version of "Connecting to Source." Enjoy!

EXERCISE 1: BREATHING & ZERO POINT

Breathing deeply allows you to re-align your cellular memory with its original blueprint. Through this exercise, you begin to align your own breath with the rhythm and pulse of the planet and the space within the earth plane and beyond.

- Close your eyes, take a deep breath in through the nose and exhale through the mouth.
- Repeat 7 to 12 times: deep breath in, exhale through the mouth.
- Ask and intend to match your breathing with the cosmic breath. Relax and enjoy.

EXERCISE 2: ASKING AND INTENDING:

You must *ask and intend* what you wish for in order for it to materialize. After taking at least 7 deep breaths, focus on your immediate intent and formulate it in this manner: "I ask and intend to feel good," "I ask and intend to feel connected and at peace," "I ask and intend to feel safe and joyful," etc.

EXERCISE 3: CREATING A SACRED SPACE

- Close your eyes, take a deep breath in through the nose and exhale through the mouth. Repeat 7 times.
- Say silently or out loud: I ask and intend to create a sacred space.
- I ask and intend that all distracting thoughts, energy and mind chatter that are not aligned with my highest good or intent

be banned from my experience and physical space now.
- I ask and intend that my Spirit Family of the highest light and who is aligned with my highest good be present with me at this time and help me create a sacred space.
- My intent is to align my energy directly with that of the Divine Source and keep my energy field sealed and protected from lower vibrations or negative influences.
- I ask and intend that my energy field remain protected and that I only experience positive flow and only that which is aligned with my highest good.
- And so it is.

EXERCISE 4: ALIGNING WITH SOURCE
- Close your eyes, take a deep breath in through the nose and exhale through the mouth. Repeat 7 times.
- I ask and intend to create a sacred space.
- I ask and intend that all distracting thoughts, energy and mind chatter that are not aligned with my highest good or intent be banned from my experience and physical space now.
- I ask and intend that my Spirit Family of the highest light and who is aligned with my highest good be present with me at this time and help me create a sacred space.
- My intent is to align my energy with that of the Divine Source.
- My intent is to bring this Source energy into my physical body, around my physical body and in this physical space.
- My intent is to experience and feel the energy of Source fill my entire being now.
- My intent is to restore my wellbeing, physically, emotionally, mentally and spiritually, as it remains aligned with the divine blueprint of Source.
- I ask and intend to maintain this perfect alignment with Source today through all that I do, see or think.
- And so it is.

After this prayer, visualize Bright Light coming down from Source (you may visualize the center of the universe or galaxy). Bring this light into your physical space above your head and let it slowly come down through the top of your head – through your crown – and then go down through your neck, filling entirely your neck, shoulders, arms, upper back, lower back, thighs, knees, ankles, and then allow the light to come out through your feet and anchor you into the Earth.

Now, visualize this Light again coming up from the Earth, through your ankles, feet, etc., all the way up and out through your crown and connecting you back to Source.

Finally, visualize that you are wrapped in a beam of Light connecting you to Heaven (Source) and Earth. Take a deep breath in (through the nose) and out (through the mouth) and bathe in this beautiful energy of Love and Light!

15

Managing Your Mind And Belief Systems

You create your reality with Mind Energy, in other words through your mind and the process of thinking. Becoming aware of the proper functioning of your mind is of utmost importance in shifting your current reality and creating the next. Here are some principles upon which your thoughts create your outer reality and experience:
- Holding any thought for a minimum of 14 seconds creates an energy cluster that automatically launches the process of creation and materialization.
- Once generated, this thought energy cluster exists within a layer of reality called the World of Probability.
- Power Controllers, and other similar beings in charge of converting energy into different forms, collect these clusters and transform them into an energy form that can materialize into physical reality.
- The actual manifestation of your thought cluster depends on the momentum it has created. The slower the momentum, the slower its manifestation. The more precise, focused and controlled your thought is, the stronger its momentum and the faster it manifests into physical reality. When your thoughts and desire do not manifest immediately, this is because the momentum created is insufficient as it is clogged with contradictory belief systems and unconscious blocks.
- Your thoughts are based on your belief systems. You enter this physical reality and engage in pre-established belief systems upon

which you base your further creativity. For example, if you believe as a child that you are not good enough, you will continue thinking and therefore creating your outer reality accordingly to the belief "I am not good enough."
- Thoughts that only affect you tend to manifest faster if there are no contradictory belief systems or unconscious blocks. Thoughts that pertain to a collective consciousness require longer to manifest because of the necessary alignment of intent of all those involved.
- Physical manifestation is based on the human creative formula (thought + desire + belief + surrender). If your thoughts are aligned with your belief system and this formula, they must and do manifest immediately.

Exercise 1: Identifying and Reversing your Belief Systems

- Close your eyes / Create a Sacred Space / Connect to Source. **See exercises 3 and 4 on page 168.**
- Bring your mind to total stillness.
- Focus on one area in your life that has not manifested to your liking. For example: finances.
- Ask and intend to clearly recognize the belief system you hold regarding finances. For example: "I have to work hard to earn money" or "it is impossible to do what I really love and earn a living at it" or "having money is corrupt" or "I simply don't deserve to be rich."
- Recognize that if you hold one of the above belief systems, then that is precisely what you will manifest.
- Ask and intend to reverse your belief systems (one at a time) by repeating the following sentences until you feel complete.

"I ask and intend to release ………………… (belief system) related to ……………… (subject) from my conscious, subconscious and cellular memory now."

"I command my subconscious to release once and for all ……………… (belief system) and replace it with a beneficial energy that is aligned with my higher good, my wellbeing and spiritual growth."

"I ask and intend that my Spirit Self, my Spirit Family and Creator to help me release once and for all .... (belief system) and replace it with beneficial energy aligned with my highest good." And so it is.
- Once you have succeeded in reversing one belief system, proceed to the next one in order of intensity. You must address all belief systems regarding the same area in order to reprogram your mind channels and begin to manifest your desire accordingly.
- After you have allowed a period of time for this mind reprogramming to take effect (approximately 14 days), proceed to the next area of your life that has not manifested to your liking. For example: career or relationships. Choose the most important area of your life and repeat the above procedure.

EXERCISE 2: Quieting Your Mind

In order to be able to discern your thoughts and achieve real mind clarity, you must be able to attain a state of total mind stillness at will. This exercise allows your channels of higher guidance and intuition to open and creates an alignment with Mind Energy of Source. It is recommended that you do this exercise for a period of at least 30 days *without interruption* until you achieve and can maintain total mind stillness for at least a few minutes. It is recommended that you continue achieving mind stillness for 5 to 10 minutes a day thereafter.

- Close your eyes / Create a Sacred Space / Connect to Source. **See exercises 3 and 4 on page 168.**
- Ask and intend to achieve total mind stillness.
- Stay focused on your breath.
- If you hear your thoughts, simply "breathe them out." You can visualize them disappearing in thin air or being swept away. If you hear yourself asking "have I achieved mind stillness?" then you have not!
- Keep trying until you succeed. You will know when you have.
- Once achieved, try to remain in that space for a few minutes.

EXERCISE 3: Experiencing the Mind Energy of Source

Mind Energy is distributed from the Divine Father at the core of your universe into your system through a light beam circuit that encircles the entire universe. This energy then pours into your planetary system and Earth through 12 main doorways or mind channels that transcend the time / space continuum. These doorways correspond to the openings located within the infinite geometrical angles and faces of your energy field. Once in your energy field, Mind Energy enters the human body through the cerebral cortex, then the limbic system, then the hypothalamus, which distributes it evenly throughout the body (through the endocrine and the nervous systems). Mind Energy's connection within the human body is the pineal gland. This energy corresponds to the mind / personality / creativity of the Divine Father. From a human perspective, it usually appears as a silverish blue color.

- Close your eyes / Create a Sacred Space / Connect to Source. **See exercises 3 and 4 on page 168.**
- Bring your mind to total stillness.
- Ask your Spirit Self and your guides to be with you and help you through this process and to remain safe and comfortable at all times.
- Bring your focus to the center of your brain, focusing on the pineal gland.
- Ask and intend to be shown how Mind Energy is distributed within your body.
- Make a note of what you have experienced and take a deep breath in and out.
- Ask and intend to focus again on your pineal gland and to be shown how Mind Energy from your head is distributed within the Earth and earth grid.
- Make a note of what you have experienced and take a deep breath in and out.
- Bring your focus again to your pineal gland and now ask to be guided upwards toward to earth grid, into the galactic core and then into the universal center.
- Once you have arrived, ask to witness and experience where

/ what Mind Energy is attached to.
- Make a note of what you have experienced and take a deep breath in and out.
- Ask to return toward the galactic center, through the earth grid, above your location and into your physical body.
- Bring your focus back into your physical body and into your heart center. Take a deep breath in and out and open your eyes.

16

Managing Your Spiritual Beliefs

While there is no such thing as one uniform way to pray, meditate or worship the Divine Creator, your current spiritual belief system may not be aligned properly with the expansion of your consciousness and the evolution of humanity. Rather than categorizing those belief systems that are positive and those that are detrimental to your growth, here are some questions that you may ask yourself regarding your current spiritual beliefs and practices:

- Do my spiritual beliefs allow me to connect with my Creator in a direct and intimate way or do I need to go through a guru, priest or spiritual teacher to reach "God?"
- Do my spiritual beliefs support the concept that I am fully responsible for creating my reality and the events in my life or am I a victim of circumstances, or do I feel a combination of both?
- Do my spiritual beliefs allow others to express and practice totally and freely their own spiritual beliefs or do I feel I need to convert them to mine, which I feel is the better way?
- Am I able to visualize and perceive myself as one aspect of the Divine Father / Mother and their extension in this physical reality or do I perceive myself as a smaller, limited being who is unable to reach divinity or the status of godhood?
- Am I able to accept my Earth journey as a pre-arranged and

agreed upon contract between myself and my Creator or do I perceive the events in my life as karmic debts or punishment so that I learn and grow?
- Do my spiritual beliefs allow me to totally master the human condition and incarnation cycle or is it impossible for me to do so in my human lifetime?
- Do my spiritual beliefs support respect and proper upkeep of my physical body (through proper nutrition and exercise) or do they impose regimented dietary restrictions, including long-term fasting and starvation?
- Do my spiritual beliefs allow me to experience life in a mature, intuitive and expanded way or must I follow regimented traditions and laws regarding my attire, ceremonies, social events and celebrations?
- Do my spiritual beliefs promote love towards all humanity regardless of political adherence, race, culture, sex or age or do my beliefs rationalize my spiritual superiority and intelligence over others?
- Do my spiritual beliefs allow me to explore other teachings and perhaps create my own or must I abide by one scripture and reject all others?
- Do my spiritual beliefs support the notion of saints, ascended masters, Sons of God, and highly evolved divine beings or am I restricted to one prophet as the only holy being?
- Do my spiritual beliefs support my intellectual, mind-al, psychic and consciousness expansion in all areas of science and cosmology or must I only operate through blind faith without the use of my psychic, mind-al or intuitive abilities?

EXERCISE 1: Experiencing Spirit Energy of Source

Spirit Energy is distributed from the Divine Mother at the core of your universe into your system evenly and transcends the time / space continuum. Spirit Energy is filtered through all the doorways of the universe and carries the breath, the rhythm and the pulse of the entire Creation within one cohesive loving energy. Spirit Energy corresponds to the nature and attributes of the Source (Love, Truth, Beauty and Goodness) and the actual person of the Infinite Spirit of

Source. Spirit Energy enters your energy field through your cerebral cortex, through your limbic system and your hypothalamus, which distributes it evenly throughout the body (through the endocrine and the nervous systems). Its connection within your body is inside the heart. From a human perspective, Spirit Energy usually appears as gold or as a soft pink and white color.

- Close your eyes / Create a Sacred Space / Connect to Source. **See exercises 3 and 4 on page 168.**
- Bring your mind to total stillness.
- Ask your Spirit Self and your guides to be with you and help you through this process and to remain safe and comfortable at all times.
- Bring your focus to the center of your heart.
- Ask and intend to be shown how Spirit Energy is distributed within your body.
- Make a note of what you have experienced and take a deep breath in and out.
- Ask and intend to focus back on your heart center and to be shown how Spirit Energy from your heart is distributed within the Earth and earth grid.
- Make a note of what you have experienced and take a deep breath in and out.
- Bring your focus back to your heart and now ask to be guided upwards through your crown chakra towards the earth grid, into the galactic core, and then into the universal center.
- Once arrived, ask to witness and experience where / what Spirit Energy is attached to.
- Make a note of what you have experienced and take a deep breath in and out.
- Ask to return towards the galactic center, through the earth grid, above your location and into your physical body.
- Bring your focus back into your physical body, your heart center, take a deep breath in and out and open your eyes.

EXERCISE 2: Identifying Your Soul Lineage and Communicating with Your Planetary or Galactic Spirit Family

Experiencing the energy and connection with your Spirit Family allows you to open your channels and awaken to your true identity and earthly purpose. It is recommended that you do this exercise once a week until clear connection and communication are mastered.

- Close your eyes / Create a Sacred Space / Connect to Source. **See exercises 3 and 4 on page 168.**
- Ask and intend to identify your individual soul lineage.
- Bring your mind to total stillness.
- Ask your Spirit Self and your guides for help, protection and safety.
- <u>Intend to remain in your physical body as you project your consciousness.</u>
- Bring your focus to your crown (top of the head).
- Visualize a beam of light coming out of your crown and begin to follow it upwards, above your physical location, your state, your country, the Earth.
- Remain within the earth plane and invoke only one of your Spirit Family (the one most appropriate to your current journey) who is <u>within the Earth plane.</u>
- Make sure you sense the presence of spirit and that you are able to identify this being's nature.
- Identify if this being is in fact present with you in this physical space or appearing to you through reflectivity.
- Ask for this being's name or a way to identify his/her identity.
- Ask your question or state your intent.
- Allow the answer to come through sensation, vision, word, letters, symbols, etc. Everything is important to note here!
- Notice how you feel during the message transmission.
- Bring back your attention and intent to your heart area and continue following the beam of light upwards towards the galactic center.
- Remain within this galaxy and invoke only one of your Spirit Family (the one most appropriate to your current journey).

- Make sure you sense a shift of energy or the presence of spirit and you are able to identify this being's nature.
- Ask for this being's name or a way to identify this being.
- Ask your question or state your intent.
- Allow the answer to come through sensation, vision, word, letters, symbols, etc. Everything is important to note here!
- Notice how you FEEL during the message transmission.
- Bring back your attention and intent to your heart area and begin to follow the light beam back downwards towards Earth.
- Ask and intend to travel towards Earth. See yourself above the earth plane, above your country, your state, your building, your physical body and slowly enter your physical body through your crown chakra.
- Ask to be anchored in your physical body. Open your eyes and write down what you have experienced.

17

Managing Your Physical Body

Your physical body is the manifestation of your Spirit and Mind Energy within physical reality. Your body is permanently attached to the Physical Energy at Source and is thus inherently self-renewed, self-managed and self-organized. While the body is a created intelligence on its own, it is continuously interacting with the outer environment as well as diverse emotions or mental stress factors. In order to sustain physical vitality as the physical body expands into higher frequencies of awakening, you must allow the body's own intelligence to self-adjust by performing a regular energetic cleanse of the endocrine system and main organs, while also supplying the body with the nourishment, rest and exercise it needs for optimum performance. In general, adopting a vegetarian organically-produced nutrition is recommended, even though occasional animal protein intake may be necessary for your temporary physiological needs. However, as the Earth transitions into higher vibrations over the next 100 years, the demands of the physical body change and allow it to receive only pure sources of minerals and organic nutrients from the Earth.

From an essence point of view, Physical Energy begins at the Source in the person of the Divine Son. It is distributed through all physical life in the universe. This energy enters the earth plane and subsequently your energy field through the cerebral cortex, the central nervous system and the skeletal system. Physical Energy's energetic connection is at the navel. From a human perspective, this energy usually appears as yellow and green.

EXERCISE 1: Experiencing Physical Energy
- Close your eyes / Create a Sacred Space / Connect to Source. **See exercises 3 and 4 on page 168.**
- Bring your mind to total stillness.
- Ask your Spirit Self and your guides to be with you and help you through this process and to remain safe and comfortable at all times.
- Bring your focus to your navel.
- Ask and intend to be shown how Physical Energy is distributed within your body.
- Make a note of what you have experienced and take a deep breath in and out.
- Ask and intend to focus back on your navel and to be shown how Physical Energy from your navel is distributed within the Earth and earth grid.
- Make a note of what you have experienced and take a deep breath in and out.
- Bring your focus back to your navel and now ask to be guided upwards through your crown towards to the earth grid, into the galactic core and then into the universal center.
- Once arrived, ask to witness and experience where / what Physical Energy is attached to.
- Make a note of what you have experienced and take a deep breath in and out.
- Ask to return towards the galactic center, through the earth grid, above your location and into your physical body.
- Bring your focus back into your physical body, your heart center, take a deep breath in and out and open your eyes.

EXERCISE 2: ENDOCRINE SYSTEM CLEANSE

It is recommended that you perform an endocrine system cleanse every 30 days.
- Close your eyes / Create a Sacred Space / Connect to Source.

See exercises 3 and 4 on page 168.

- Bring your mind to total stillness.
- Ask your Spirit Self and your guides to be with you and help you through this process and to remain safe and comfortable at all times.
- Bring your focus to the pineal gland (middle of the brain). Ask to identify any disturbance or imbalance in this area. You may perceive a faded color or experience a negative emotion.
- Ask to reverse, restore or heal any imbalance or negative emotion in the pineal gland.
- Take a deep breath in through the nose, out through the mouth.
- Bring your focus to the pituitary gland (middle of the brain). Ask to identify any disturbance or imbalance in this area. You may perceive a faded color or experience a negative emotion.
- Ask to reverse, restore or heal any imbalance or negative emotion in the pituitary gland.
- Take a deep breath in through the nose, out through the mouth.
- Bring your focus to the thyroid glands (throat area). Ask to identify any disturbance or imbalance in this area. You may perceive a faded color or experience a negative emotion.
- Ask to reverse, restore or heal any imbalance or negative emotion in the thyroid glands.
- Take a deep breath in through the nose, out through the mouth.
- Bring your focus to the thymus gland (chest area, behind the heart). Ask to identify any disturbance or imbalance in this area. You may perceive a faded color or experience a negative emotion.
- Ask to reverse, restore or heal any imbalance or negative

emotion in the thymus gland.
- Take a deep breath in through the nose, out through the mouth.
- Bring your focus to the pancreas gland (left stomach area). Ask to identify any disturbance or imbalance in this area. You may perceive a faded color or experience a negative emotion.
- Ask to reverse, restore or heal any imbalance or negative emotion in the pancreas gland.
- Take a deep breath in through the nose, out through the mouth.
- Bring your focus to the adrenal glands (middle of the back above the kidneys) Ask to identify any disturbance or imbalance in this area. You may perceive a faded color or experience a negative emotion.
- Ask to reverse, restore or heal any imbalance or negative emotion in the adrenal glands.
- Take a deep breath in through the nose, out through the mouth.
- Bring your focus to the ovaries or testes glands (uterus / groin area). Ask to identify any disturbance or imbalance in this area. You may perceive a faded color or experience a negative emotion.
- Ask to reverse, restore or heal any imbalance or negative emotion in the ovaries or testes glands.

EXERCISE 3: PHYSICAL ORGANS FLUSH

An organ flush is recommended once every 30 days. Focus on the following organs or those that are bothering you at that time: head, brain, spinal cord, lungs, heart, stomach, intestines, colon, liver, spleen, kineys, skeleton (include muscles and tissues).

- Close your eyes / Create a Sacred Space / Connect to Source.

See exercises 3 and 4 on page 168.
- Bring your mind to total stillness.
- Ask your Spirit Self and your guides to be with you and help you through this process and to remain safe and comfortable at all times.
- Bring your focus to your entire head. Ask to identify any disturbance or imbalance in this area. You may perceive a faded color or experience a negative emotion.
- Ask to reverse, restore or heal any imbalance or negative emotion in your head.
- Take a deep breath in through the nose, out through the mouth.
- Bring your focus to your brain. Ask to identify any disturbance or imbalance in this area. You may perceive a faded color or experience a negative emotion.
- Ask to reverse, restore or heal any imbalance or negative emotion in the brain.
- Take a deep breath in through the nose, out through the mouth.
- Bring your focus to your spine. Ask to identify any disturbance or imbalance in this area. You may perceive a faded color or experience a negative emotion.
- Ask to reverse, restore or heal any imbalance or negative emotion in the spine.
- Take a deep breath in through the nose, out through the mouth.
- Bring your focus to your lungs. Ask to identify any disturbance or imbalance in this area. You may perceive a faded color or experience a negative emotion.
- Ask to reverse, restore or heal any imbalance or negative emotion in the lungs.
- Take a deep breath in through the nose, out through the mouth.
- Bring your focus to your physical heart. Ask to identify any disturbance or imbalance in this area. You may perceive a faded color or experience a negative emotion.
- Ask to reverse, restore or heal any imbalance or negative

emotion in the heart.
- Take a deep breath in through the nose, out through the mouth.
- Bring your focus to the stomach. Ask to identify any disturbance or imbalance in this area. You may perceive a faded color or experience a negative emotion.
- Ask to reverse, restore or heal any imbalance or negative emotion in the stomach.
- Take a deep breath in through the nose, out through the mouth.
- Bring your focus to your liver. Ask to identify any disturbance or imbalance in this area. You may perceive a faded color or experience a negative emotion.
- Ask to reverse, restore or heal any imbalance or negative emotion in the liver.
- Take a deep breath in through the nose, out through the mouth.
- Bring your focus to your intestines and colon. Ask to identify any disturbance or imbalance in this area. You may perceive a faded color or experience a negative emotion.
- Ask to reverse, restore or heal any imbalance or negative emotion in the intestines and colon.
- Bring your focus to your spleen. Ask to identify any disturbance or imbalance in this area. You may perceive a faded color or experience a negative emotion.
- Ask to reverse, restore or heal any imbalance or negative emotion in the spleen.
- Take a deep breath in through the nose, out through the mouth.
- Bring your focus to your kidneys. Ask to identify any disturbance or imbalance in this area. You may perceive a faded color or experience a negative emotion.
- Ask to reverse, restore or heal any imbalance or negative emotion in the kidneys.
- Take a deep breath in through the nose, out through the mouth.
- Bring your focus to your skeleton (include your muscle and

tissues). Ask to identify any disturbance or imbalance in this area. You may perceive a faded color or experience a negative emotion.
- Ask to reverse, restore or heal any imbalance or negative emotion in the skeleton, muscles and tissues.
- Take a deep breath in through the nose, out through the mouth.

18

Managing Your Career

In these times of great planetary change, many are struggling to align with their true divine purpose or calling while also attending to their immediate material needs, which are being met, to a certain extent, by conventional occupations such as accounting, sales, marketing, information technology, etc. Others are finding themselves unable to manifest to their liking work that seems fulfilling or aligned with their inner truth. Regardless of your unique circumstances, you must become aware of the impact your current career – or the lack of it – has on your spirit and mind expansion. Once this awareness has been achieved, a sound decision can be made regarding manifesting a new career or remaining status quo with the one you have, while applying the principles discussed in this book. In other words, not only is it not mandatory to leave a seemingly limited conventional work in order to manifest your true calling, but it may be that your true calling has already manifested through this particular occupation in the sense that you may be bringing forth your enlightened vision to the field you are currently occupying. By choosing to remain in your current job, you may begin to implement your higher knowledge and awakened energy within your workplace simply through energy transfer. You may be raising others' vibration around you simply by routinely interacting with them or sharing the same physical space. However, if these interactions become intolerable as your higher vibrations emerge, then it may certainly become an appropriate measure to pursue other options that are more aligned with your true purpose.

Whether you remain in your current situation or begin to actively work in a new area of your choice, aligning properly with the energies surfacing on the earth plane is important. In order to do so, you may want to observe the following guidelines:

1. Ask and intend each day that you bring into your workplace the highest vibration possible for yourself and for others around you.

2. Ask and intend each day that you remain focused on a global, humanitarian and altruistic awareness.

3. Ask and intend to bring joy, love, truth and goodness into your workplace whether others are displaying it or not.

4. Ask and intend that your work keeps stimulating your mind and spirit and allows you to excel in all areas so that you may reflect the same onto others.

5. Ask and intend to bring the highest level of morality and integrity into your workplace.

6. Ask and intend to bring environmental awareness into your workplace and into all that you do, think or say.

7. Ask and intend to spread healing and raise the consciousness of all those with whom you come in contact.

EXERCISE 1: Reversing Fears and Subconscious Blocks Related to Career

- Close your eyes / Create a Sacred Space / Connect to Source. **See exercises 3 and 4 on page 168.**
- Bring your mind to total stillness.
- Ask your Spirit Self and your guides to be with you and help you through this process and to remain safe and comfortable at all times.
- Repeat the following sentences until you feel complete:

"I ask and intend to release all my fears and subconscious blocks related to manifesting the career and work that is aligned with

my highest divine purpose from my conscious, subconscious and cellular memory now."

"I command my subconscious to release once and for all my fears and blocks related to manifesting my highest work and replace them with a beneficial energy that is aligned with my higher good, my wellbeing and spiritual growth."

"I ask and intend my Spirit Self, my Spirit Family and Creator to help me release once and for all my fears and subconscious blocks related to manifesting the work that is aligned with my highest divine purpose and replace them with beneficial energy aligned with my highest good."

"And so it is."

EXERCISE 2: Receiving Clarity and Manifesting your Physical Work

- Close your eyes / Create a Sacred Space / Connect to Source. **See exercises 3 and 4 on page 168.**
- Bring your mind to total stillness.
- Ask your Spirit Self and your guides to be with you and help you through this process and to remain safe and comfortable at all times.
- Repeat the following sentences until you feel complete:

"I ask and intend that my Spirit Self offers me clarity in the area of my career or creative expression, so I may make the proper decisions that are aligned with my higher good and that of others."

"I ask and intend to attract ideas, individuals and circumstances that will allow me to manifest and expand the work that is aligned with my higher purpose."

"I ask and intend that my work be in line with my spiritual growth, mind expansion and improve my physical life so I may enrich my life and that of others."

"I am grateful for the work and career opportunities I have created so far and ask to manifest those that allow me to manifest my higher and divine purpose."

"And so it is."

19

Managing Your Home Life

The tremendous new shifts bring inevitable governmental, economical, astrological and geophysical changes that may disrupt our daily life. Many are questioning the location of their current home and the need to possibly relocate in order to avoid being part of these disruptions. This book clarifies that many geographical areas are to be affected one way or another, directly or indirectly, so disruptions may occur in a variety of ways. Ironically, some areas will experience awakenings as the Earth takes them into the deeper disturbances. At this juncture, however, it is important to realize that whatever is about to alter the geophysicality of the planet will be globally felt, ranging from minor to more debilitating ways. It is appropriate and important to prepare for such events accordingly.

It is recommended to remain aligned and connected *at all times* with the highest guiding power on the planet, the one orchestrating such massive movements on a global scale and that is the Divine Source. By asking to be continuously aligned with the Divine Plan of Source, you will be automatically spared the drastic fragmentations of the Earth and will not incur severe repercussions or threats to your well-being. You may need, however, to be prepared to alter your daily life in the spur of a moment and this includes collecting food and water supplies for prolonged periods of time or temporarily relocating to safer grounds. While there may not be any harm to your immediate being, discomforts such as the interruption of communication or transportation services may hinder your routine. By remaining connected to Source, whether you are capable of retrieving guidance with clarity or not, your wellbeing and the wellbeing of your loved ones will be safeguarded at all times.

EXERCISE 1: Remaining Protected and Guided in the Period of Earth Changes

Repeat as often as desired until you feel complete.
- I ask and intend to remain aligned perfectly with the energy of the Divine Source and the energy of the Divine Creator, the One orchestrating the tremendous changes on our planet.
- I ask and intend to remain safe and protected during the times of earth disruption. I ask and intend that all those I know personally and humanity at large also be safe and protected.
- I ask and intend that my Spirit Self and Spirit Family be with me at all times. I ask and intend to receive guidance with clarity and precision regarding the appropriate measures that I can take to alleviate the physical discomforts that may disrupt my daily life.
- I ask and intend to remain trusting and loving during times of severe changes and to uphold a lucid and collected mental and emotional state in order to allow my higher good and the higher good of others to manifest.
- I trust that all that happens is aligned with the Divine Plan, the highest good of humanity and the planet and I ask to be an instrument and vessel of this light through all that I think, say or do, especially in those moments of severe disruptions.
- And so it is.

20

Managing Your Family Life And Friends

Relationships with fiends and family are a continuous challenge for many. However, when humanity is facing massive changes and the annihilation of existing realities, we are ready to assist even those who trigger in us constant grief and anxiety. This includes those close family members and friends who remain oblivious to the inevitable changes manifesting on the earth plane in the years to come. While we must safeguard our own connection and strength during these times, we cannot help but be concerned with others. Subsequently, our own energy field gets distorted and fragmented as we stretch ourselves to save another. It is important to realize that each and every being in human form is currently creating their own reality (through their Spirit Self), whether his/her conscious / human mind seems awakened or not, whether he/she has full cognitive capacity or not. During sleep, the Spirit Self becomes aware of the approaching waves of planetary transformation, and, even though this information may not be complete or clearly defined, everyone, without exception, carefully chooses to manifest what his/her soul needs to experience during these times. Therefore, a certain level of allowing and trusting is necessary to deal with this important quandary.

On the other hand, it is also important to resolve all issues, including those pertaining to relationships. If these issues are triggering anxiety, fear, anger or confusion, this is for the purpose of resolving these issues within us. It is best to take the person triggering such emotions or blocks out of the equation and to observe the nature or content of the issue in relation to our own growth. For example, if your mother triggers anxiety within you, first ignore the aspect of your mother. Then, ask to see why anxiety is being triggered in you at this time and what the best way to reverse it or heal it may be. Keep in mind that such emotions are not only normal but also necessary as a warning bell or alarm as you interact with the physical worlds. However, when the same emotion is recurrent in all that you do and in all circumstances then this emotion becomes a block that needs to be addressed and healed. Here are some exercises and tips to begin healing fully all your relationships, including the ones that appear impossible to handle.

EXERCISE 1: Healing the Wounds of a Relationship

Focus on only one relationship at a time when doing this exercise. Identify the emotions associated with this person and situation in Part I (for example: I am angry, frustrated, etc.). Then identify the belief system associated with this person and situation in Part II (for example: "I don't believe this person is capable of change" or "I don't believe this relationship can be salvaged").

- Close your eyes / Create a Sacred Space / Connect to Source. **See exercises 3 and 4 on page 168.**
- Bring your mind to total stillness.
- Ask your Spirit Self and your guides to be with you and help you through this process and to remain safe and comfortable at all times.

Part I:
- Repeat the following affirmation for each emotion regarding this person:

"I ask and intend to release my .... (emotion) towards .... (person)."

- Take a deep breath in through the nose and out through the mouth.

Part II:
- Repeat the following statement for each belief system associated with this person:

"I ask and intend to release .... (belief system) related to .... (subject) from my conscious, subconscious and cellular memory now."

"I command my subconscious to release once and for all .... (belief system) and replace it with a beneficial energy that is aligned with my higher good, my wellbeing and spiritual growth."

"I ask and intend my Spirit Self, my Spirit Family and Creator to help me with releasing once and for all .... (belief system) and replace it with beneficial energy aligned with my highest good."

"And so it is."

EXERCISE 2: Prayer for Healthy Relationships
- Close your eyes / Create a Sacred Space / Connect to Source. **See exercises 3 and 4 on page 168.**
- Bring your mind to total stillness.
- Ask your Spirit Self and your guides to be with you and help you through this process and to remain safe and comfortable at all times.
- Repeat the following affirmation for each emotion regarding this person:

"I ask and intend that I get along with .... as best as possible and to resolve our differences in love and harmony."

"I ask and intend to be responsible for my own emotions and experiences and refrain from blame or victimization from past experiences."

"I ask and intend to release all negative emotions pertaining to .... (incident) or .... (person) so I may be free mentally and emotionally."

"I ask and intend to forgive myself for .... (experience) as well as .... (person associated with

incident) and acknowledge that I and .... are both spiritually whole and perfect. I acknowledge that the past actions of .... may have been misguided or inappropriate and ask for their emotional recovery and release."

"I ask and intend to give and receive love from now on and share a harmonious and loving relationship with ...."

"I ask and intend that this relationship be effortless and in perfect alignment with both our spiritual paths and our mind/soul expansion."

"I ask and intend that this relationship be an uplifting daily co-creation and a joyful and positive experience for both."

"I ask and intend that my relationship with .... be a daily reminder reflection of the loving spirit of the Divine Creator."

"And so it is."

Final Note

If you can agree that you are a Divine Being in human form, then you shall become one.

Glossary

Aspect: Part of a divine entity or being.

Bestowal: Dispensation.

Creator Energy: Energy of the Divine Creator (Divine Father and Divine Mother) of the Local Universe, similar to the concept of "Christ Consciousness."

Creator-Source: Original Creator of All That Is – all of existence.

Creator Order: Order of intelligent beings capable of creating universes, planets and other species.

Divine Blueprint: Divine "DNA" formula as originally created by the Divine Creator of the Local Universe.

Divine Father Of The Central Universe: Original Creator of a Major Universe, which contains over 100,000 Local Universes. He is also the original Creator of all intelligent beings and species within the Central Universe.

Divine Father Of The Local Universe: Original Creator of the Local Universe and all intelligent beings and species therein.

Divine Geometry: Geometry based on infinite mathematical numbers, equations, sequence and shapes.

Divine Master: Beings of the ascending or descending order who have mastered the human condition through physical incarnation.

Divine Mother: Original co-Creator of life within the Local Universe, which includes all intelligent beings and species.

Divine Son: Aspect of the Divine Creator, also Physical Energy, that is able to manifest in human and other forms on the many worlds within the Local Universe.

Dodecahedron: A geometric shape that has 12 regular pentagonal faces, 20 vertices and 30 edges.

Evolutionary Beings: Intelligent beings who must incarnate in material from, human or otherwise, in order to expand their consciousness. Even though all types of intelligent beings are created by the Divine Creator at the core of the Local Universe, each created being is then transported to a new world which becomes their place of origin or "home."

Feminine Energy: Feminine aspects or attributes that can be embodied by both male and female material beings.

Invisible Physical Beings: Beings from other planetary systems who inhabit the earth plane but exist in another layer of reality (frequency range) and thereby remain invisible to the human eye.

Life Architects: Beings of the 4th Creator Order who are in charge of producing new life forms and implanting them on the various worlds.

Major Universe: Universal structure that contains over 100,000 Local Universes.

Material Beings: Intelligent beings of the evolutionary order who may be human or non-human, from the earth plane or other planets.

Melchizedeks: Universal Beings of the highest Teacher Order.

Mind Energy: Aspect of the Creator-Source, personalized as the Universal Father and subsequently the Divine Father, that is responsible for the creation of consciousness and the collection of thoughts.

Perpetual Unit Circle: The perpetual circle is not finite but rather a circle that continuously recreates itself. After the completion of one circle or cycle, each subsequent circle re-generation is never exactly identical to the previously created one.

Physical Energy: Aspect of the Creator-Source, personalized by the Universal Son and subsequently the Divine Son, responsible for the creation of all physical energy and physical life in existence.

Platonic Solids: 3-dimensional aspects of the Polygon. All these shapes' sides, edges and angles are congruent.

Power Controllers: Powerful divine beings who remain in spirit form and are responsible for maneuvering energy.

Principle: Attribute of a divine entity or being.

Reflectivity: Universal law that allows energetic information to be transferred from one point to another and be perceived by, retrieved and understood fully by the receiver without the use of a common language.

Sea Of Glass: Area within the Central Universe and all Local Universes resembling a massive stadium where inter-galactic and trans-universal information is transferred through the process of reflectivity.

Seraphic Order: Beings of the angelic realm who offer guidance and protection for humanity.

Spirit Energy: Aspect of the Creator-Source, personalized as the Universal Spirit and subsequently the Divine Mother, that is responsible for sustaining the pulse, breath and life force within Creation.

Spirit Family: Stream of consciousness comprised of beings in material or spirit form who share the same lineage.

Spirit Self: The aspect of the self that remains permanently connected with Source.

World Of Probability: Frequency range where thoughts are accumulated in order to reach enough momentum to allow material manifestation.

Zero Point: Areas within physical space and throughout Creation that allow the collapse, recreation, transmutation and regeneration of energy.

Acknowledgments

*To the Divine Assembly of 7 and 12, the Divine Sons and Masters,
My Divine Brothers Gabriel, Edwar, Antoine,
And to all the Masters in human form….
Thank you!*